Painless Mental Math:

Quick, Easy, and Useful Ways to Become a Human Calculator (Even if You Suck at Math)

By Peter Hollins, Author and Researcher at petehollins.com

Table of Contents

Chapter 1. "I *hate* math!" 9
   Math Anxiety 17
   The Social Stigma on Math 19
   Developing a Growth Mindset 21
   Takeaways 27

Chapter 2. Mental Math in Daily Life 30
   Math in Shopping 35
   Math at Home 46
   Math at School 50
   Math and Food 54
   Miscellaneous Math Concepts and Their Applications 60
   Takeaways 62

Chapter 3. Calculations 65
   Mentally multiplying large numbers 67
   Adding and subtracting fractions using the Butterfly Method 68
   Reverse-Zorro Method 69
   Memorize simple arithmetic 70
   Find a square number slightly bigger than the biggest one you know 72
   Obtaining the square of a two-digit number ... 73
   Divisibility tests 73
      Divisibility by 4 74
      Divisibility by 6 75
      Divisibility by 7 75

Divisibility by 8 76
Decimal representations 76
　　11ths 77
　　9ths 77
Mentally adding numbers 77
Mentally subtracting numbers 78
Subtracting from 1,000 79
Squares are your friends 80
Squaring numbers that end in 5 81
Approximating a square root 82
Binomial Theorem for squaring 82
Scientific notation for huge numbers 83
Handy multiplication tricks 83
Complex multiplication 84
Multiplying 5 times any number 85
Multiplying by 9 86
Multiply by 11 87
Multiplying numbers that end in zero 87
FOIL method for multiplication 88
Multiply by rounding 89
Mental Math: the skills of calculating fast. 89
　　1) Offensive. 89
　　2) Defensive. 90
　　3) Entertaining. 91
Percentages 91
Switching percentages 92
Miscellaneous calculation methods 92
Takeaways 100

Chapter 4. Vedic Math 105
Sutra 1: Ekadhikena Purvena (By one more than the previous one) 112

Sutra 2: Nikhilam Navatashcaramam Dashatah (All from 9 and the last from 10) 115
Sutra 3: Urdhva-Tiryagbhyam (Vertically and crosswise) 116
   Multiplying numbers close to 10 117
   Multiplying numbers close to 100 118
   Multiplying numbers just over 100. 119
   Using the sutra to add and subtract fractions 120
Sutra 4: Shunyam Saamyasamuccaye (When the sum is the same that sum is zero) 121
Sutra 5: Gyarasguna Sutra (One number can be easily multiplied by 11) 123
Sutra 6: Paravartya Yojayet (Transpose and adjust) 125
Sutra 7: Anurupyena-Sunyamanyat (If one is in a ratio, the other is zero) 128
Sutra 8: Sankalana-Vyavakalanabhyam (By addition and subtraction) 130
Sutra 9: Puranapuranabyham (By the completion or non-completion) 131
Sutra 10: Yaavadunam (Whatever the extent of its deficiency) 133
Sutra 11: Vyashtisamanstih (Part and whole) 134
Sutra 12: Shesanyankena Charamena (The remainders by the last digit) 135
Sutra 13: Sopaantyadvayamantyam (The ultimate and twice the penultimate) 138
Sutra 14: Ekanyunena Purvena (By one less than the previous one) 139

Sutra 15: Gunitasamuchyah (The product of the sum is equal to the sum of the product) 140

Sutra 16: Gunakasamuchyah (The factors of the sum are equal to the sum of the factors) 141

Takeaways 142

Chapter 5. The Trachtenberg System........ 145
Multiplication using the Trachtenberg System 152

   Multiplying two digits with two digits 152
   Multiplying any number with a two-digit number........................ 156
   Multiplying a number with a 3-digit number 158
   Using Multipliers of Any Length......................... 161

Addition in Trachtenberg's System 164

Verifying your answer 171

Division in the Trachtenberg System 172

Takeaways 180

Summary Guide 183

Chapter 1. "I *hate* math!"

The prospect of even basic mathematics can provoke debilitating fear unlike anything else. Math is easily the most hated subject in school and college curricula, and it is common to hear students complaining about how difficult and uninteresting math is, or how much they despise attending math lectures. Count me as one of those people! For those still in school, there are four main reasons for this.

First, there are a limited number of ways to earn good grades in math. Scoring 100 percent on a math-based question relies on you getting the right answer, which isn't subjective like in the case of subjects such as English. Often, you will get points for following the right procedure or steps on a given problem, but there are several ways to solve a question and you might not get credit for some methods.

Second, students also perceive math to be dull. The way teachers present math concepts is crucial to the way students perceive the subject. Too often, they're left with the impression that math is an abstract subject with no practical applications. It's filled with a random assortment of numbers that can be difficult to grasp unless you're intimately familiar with the subject, which most math-averse students are not.

Third, students think math requires too much memorization: The memorization in math mainly pertains to the various formulas one needs to apply to solve questions. However, when learning topics like calculus, there can be hundreds of formulas that are all considered important. The part often missed here is that most of these formulas can be derived intuitively if one understands the logic underlying them.

Leaving out this intuitive process is one weakness in conventional math teaching methods.

Lastly, learning math generally requires making mistakes: Jules Verne once said, "Science, my lad, is made up of mistakes, but they are mistakes which it is useful to make because little by little they lead us to the truth." Math too is a science, and it is only by making mistakes that one learns the correct methods of doing math. However, most students are discouraged by the mistakes they make, and it is important to balance that with positive affirmations and encouragement toward learning the subject.

The scorn for math is far from restricted to school or college students. The affliction is common in humans of all ages, long after they've graduated from their respective institutions. This points toward the fact that it is not just the way math is taught in schools that instills this fear of the subject, but also certain features of math itself.

Learning math is like learning a new language.

It has its own symbols that interact with numbers or letters in unique ways which we don't use in our ordinary lives. For the uninitiated, math can be a tangle of rules and methods that don't solve the problems of our everyday lives. Some of these connections are highly abstract and beneficial only for those intending to specialize in the natural sciences. Much of what we would utilize in our daily lives is not nearly as complicated, but once someone grasps the internal logic governing the basic calculations, transitioning toward more complex math becomes easier.

However, what stops most from making that transition, or even attempting to understand mathematical concepts at all, is the fact that it is socially acceptable, even beneficial, to hate math. If you were to joke about disliking math at a gathering, you need not worry about appearing stupid in the same way as you would if you had said you dislike history or English.

Instead, you often generate laughs or empathy because everyone around you, even those fond of mathematical logic, has experienced the frustrations the subject causes. These frustrations are key in the perception of math as a subject reserved for nerds, and since nobody wants to be associated with nerds, they either avoid math like a plague or joke about how cumbersome it is.

Much of this unwieldiness has to do with finding that elusive value of x which every question seeks to discover. People who like math enjoy the satisfaction they derive from having braved the logical labyrinth that any math question creates. But others often struggle to find any good reason to care about what x is. They seek a reward for doing math, and deducing the value of x is simply not enough since they don't see how calculating for x in theory can help them find x in real-life situations.

Having said that, there is also a deficiency in communicating math in an accessible manner. This is, in no minor part, because of its aforementioned abstract nature. Questions, explanations, and theories can be phrased in notoriously ambiguous ways that make them appear obscure and unnecessarily difficult. The mathematicians who frame them aren't usually the most adept at linguistics, or even at just being able to make things simpler for everyone. The students trying to decipher the experts' convoluted language are the first to suffer.

Another reason why most people don't bother with the complexities of math nowadays is that we all have calculators in our pocket since we all own smartphones. Why bother doing calculations when a device can do them for you? Calculators are also quicker, and the process only takes a few seconds. While this is a compelling argument, and the use of calculators is highly convenient in our daily lives, it misses the point of doing math.

To be fair, even engineers, scientists and mathematicians themselves rely on calculators; with a range from the simple calculators in our smartphones to those of supercomputers. They need these machines to perform large-scale calculations that will take a human a lifetime to accomplish.

However, math isn't simply about finding the right answer. It's about applying logic in valid ways to proceed from one step to another. Calculators can rob us of the joy of arriving independently at an answer from our own mental efforts by eliminating the process and reducing it to an input and output of values. We can excuse specialists with their use of computers for advanced calculations.

But for everyone who is studying the basics, being able to do the mathematical calculations ourselves also reduces our unnecessary dependence on technology. While our phones are practically attached to our bodies, calculators breed a culture wherein children are afraid to rely on themselves for even basic addition or subtraction. More than that, they further exacerbate the already entrenched notion that math is simply all about the results.

Our logic and creativity are two essential traits that make us human and distinct from animals. And yes, creativity is indispensable to mathematics, contrary to commonly held belief. The constant reliance on calculators prevents us from developing those qualities.

The flip side to this is a quote from Karate Kid, "There is no such thing as a bad student, only a bad teacher." Bad teachers are notorious for instilling fear for particular subjects amongst students from an early age, and this is especially the case with math, where the standard of teaching needs to be higher. When a child fails to do math well, teachers and even parents often interpret this as a damning verdict on the child's possession of analytical faculties.

The truth is that teachers often make up for their own inadequacies by blaming the child for their failure to learn. This causes many parents to opt for private tutoring to ensure that their children don't lag behind in the subject, but this can come with its own additional pressures to perform well, something that ultimately breeds contempt and loathing for math as a subject.

Math Anxiety

Most of us are intuitively aware of the various reasons why math is difficult, and why so many struggle with it. However, the sheer horror that math can evoke has caused many of us to become the subject of ridicule for what is perceived as an exaggerated reaction to a minor issue. If this is something you have experienced, it isn't all in your head. The spectrum of the mental disorder of anxiety has a myriad of triggers. In some cases, math can be one of them. There is now ample research to support the phenomenon of math anxiety, wherein the prospect of doing math can cause adverse physiological symptoms.

From a physiological perspective, students with high levels of math anxiety have been found to have more active amygdalae—a part of the brain tasked with processing negative emotions and fearful stimuli. At the same time, sections of the brain responsible for mathematical processing are less active in these students. Thus, math anxiety is a real phenomenon with observable effects on our minds and bodies that can be crippling for those suffering from it.

There's more to math anxiety than simply the prospect of having to do math. It is never an overstatement to say that, in itself, mathematics is not something to be afraid of. There are some specific reasons that cause individuals to be overly anxious about math, and these can be ingrained into children from a very young age.

Chief among these is a fear of being wrong. Students can often be mocked or laughed at by their peers for failing to get the right answer to a question—and in math, unlike other subjects, there is only one correct answer. Alternatively, failing at a question might lower their confidence and make them unwilling to even try again. This unwillingness becomes an attitude that is adopted whenever something appears too complicated, and can have a negative impact on their chances of academic or real-world success. The pressure exerted during a timed test only exacerbates this fear of being wrong, since there is less time to rectify errors.

Other common reasons include children having parents who are negatively predisposed toward math, either due to their own experience with the subject or the fact that they haven't needed it for their success. This not only discourages interest in the subject, but makes it more acceptable for children to dislike math.

One of the most effective steps you can take is reinforcing a supportive learning environment (like what this book provides).

The Social Stigma on Math

The discussion on math anxiety so far treats it as an internal issue that some of us suffer from due to our unique individual problems. However, it is important to point out that society and culture are significantly formative to our inner psychological makeup. In fact, recent research shows that much of the stigma surrounding math is socially enforced, and often has precious little to do with one's own deficiencies.

An example of this is that girls are perceived to be weaker at math than boys due to their respective mental composition. But a study published by the Notices of the American Mathematical Society suggests a different reason for the discrepancy. It concludes that the reason girls often perform worse at math is because of social pressures that make them shun the subject.

Researchers behind this study analyzed the cultural backgrounds of the best-performing college and high school students who participate in math competitions. prized as an important and useful skill. Being adept at math was thus a source of prestige. These students or their parents primarily hailed from Asian or Eastern European countries, exposing them to non-American attitudes toward math. Given that girls from these countries excelled at math, the researchers suggested that females don't have any inherent deficiency stunting their mathematical ability. Rather, girls in the US are simply socially conditioned to view the subject negatively.

Developing a Growth Mindset

All of the aforementioned factors generally combine to make us feel powerless when it comes to learning math. They believe that mathematical ability is a biological trait or an innate gift that they have simply been deprived of. This leads to a polarized and fatalistic perception of math as something people are either excellent or terrible at. Such ideas can be deep-seated and difficult to change, especially due to the rigors of learning the subject.

This is where the concept of the *growth mindset* becomes relevant. Growth mindset is all about the capacity and motivation for personal development. It is the belief that there is always room for improvement, and the ability to do so. Its underlying philosophy looks at people as having control over their skill set.

Framing human learning—math, in particular—within the growth mindset paradigm instills the belief that our minds grow and change as we gain experience, that students don't possess a static set of strengths and weaknesses. It is a perspective that can help encourage students and children to learn from their mistakes and devise new methods to approach problems through positive reinforcement and encouragement.

A portion of this series is specifically geared toward math teachers. A crucial aspect of the approach is the attempt to normalize failure through methods such as sharing incorrect answers with peers, or encouraging students to ask questions they would normally be afraid to raise. Mistakes are regarded here as a normal and necessary part of a student's pursuit of learning. The point is that making a mistake in solving math problems is a step forward, not an obstacle, and it is never a reason to give up.

An example that applies the approach involves a daily activity called "*my favorite no.*" For this exercise, teachers have their students solve a problem daily on an index card at the beginning of class before sorting the answers into correct and incorrect piles. They must then copy an incorrect answer onto the board and ask students to identify its correct elements before focusing on the part of the solution that ultimately led to the erroneous answer. This is beneficial even for those children that initially got the right answer, since they can learn from the mistakes of their peers.

In lieu with the growth mindset paradigm, it is important for teachers to devise innovative ways to teach math in order to facilitate better learning. It is only through an effective teaching method that we can cultivate a growth mindset among learners. Otherwise, students will be inclined to believe that even sustained effort on their part is insufficient for grasping math.

One of the ways in which teachers can avoid discouragement is to utilize "*open problems*," which emphasize understanding concepts rather than simply discovering the solution to a given problem. This enables students to explore the different methods at their disposal to solve math exercises, minimizing judgement based on whether their answers are correct.

An example is to ask students how many baseballs would be needed to fill up their classroom. This compels them to determine the information they would require to begin answering this question. Once they've arrived at the answer, ask them how it would change if the dimensions of the room were to be expanded. Their work highlights the importance of the process of getting to the correct answer, along with clarifying how different concepts are related to each other.

Unfortunately, a culture that impedes growth mindset rules over many areas of human endeavor. Education is no exception. General methods of teaching math often sacrifice the process in favor of achieving the right answer. This isn't to say that we should simply throw away pre-existing methods. What we need is to restore the lost balance between the two: the results-based and process-based approaches. *Open problem* is one such approach that addresses this matter.

The Sun conducted some research relating to this and gauged the mindset of 3,400 students along with forty teachers. They also assessed the attitudes of the teachers—whether they valued speed or memorization versus multi-dimensional problems that allow for critical thinking. Based on observations, they concluded that teachers who utilized multi-dimensional problems were more likely to have students with a growth mindset.

Many of the teachers tutoring children have themselves learned math in traditional ways that did not encourage critical thinking. It is thus imperative for them to examine their own attitudes and teaching methods to maximize learning amongst their students.

The polar opposite of the growth mindset is the *fixed mindset*. Most of us have this tendency more than we would like to admit. This type of mindset is characterized by a rigid attitude toward skill sets. It is the belief that attributes are fixed and unchangeable, for better or for worse.

Talent is everything and effort is unnecessary.

Even after being aware of the benefits of a growth mindset, we might struggle to dispel our preconceived notions about subjects like math. After all, the social conditioning that informs our beliefs can be traced far back to childhood. Whatever the case, this mindset is potentially dangerous because it stunts your ability to grow and learn new skills, which has significant consequences for your success and happiness later in life.

For example, if you perceive yourself to be someone who isn't proficient at math, that simply acts as an excuse for you to avoid practicing it. Though it might prevent the disappointment of failure in the short-term, believing it is acceptable to avoid topics we're not well-versed with hinders long-term growth and development. Carol Dweck, a researcher at Stanford University, has conducted extensive research on the subject of how our beliefs affect our performance. Through her work, she has concluded that the best way to modify negative personal beliefs is through small, repeated actions that align with the identity you want to build for yourself.

These actions also shift the way one perceives math as a subject, since your inability to do math relies on a specific, albeit inaccurate, preconception of what math is. Contrary to the general notion that math is practically irrelevant, this subject pervades our everyday life in several interesting and thought-provoking ways. To see this, you simply need to complete some basic math tasks repeatedly that change how you perceive both math as a discipline and your proficiency at it.

Takeaways

It is no secret that math is among the most reviled subjects taught to us in school. There are many reasons for this, from poor teaching methods, to the impression that the subject lacks practical applicability, and the ever-present choice of simply using a calculator instead. The extent of our hatred for math has reached such heights that math anxiety is now a commonly recognized phenomenon wherein just the prospect of having to do math causes adverse mental and physiological symptoms.

All of these factors have combined to make math skills a reason to be socially ostracized. Math is perceived to be a subject only fit for the nerdiest of nerds. It just isn't cool, and if one is good at it, their analytical acumen is thought to be a sign of abnormality. The result of such attitudes is that mathematical ability is perceived to be a purely natural skill that one is either born with in spades, or has been robbed of due to the vagaries of cosmic justice. Students who struggle with math are stuck believing they are doomed to be unsuccessful at the subject no matter how much effort they put into improving their skills.

Teachers are thus tasked with reversing the trend and inculcating a growth mindset in their students by normalizing failure and providing ample encouragement instead of derision. When children are placed in supportive teaching environments that don't punish them for an inability to solve every problem, while also providing them with innovative and interesting ways to learn, their attitudes toward math change. Their improvements reinforce the belief that math is something anybody can excel at when provided with the necessary resources.

Chapter 2. Mental Math in Daily Life

One of the main difficulties students face while learning math is struggling to apply it practically in their daily lives. The pervasive negative attitudes surrounding math reinforce the notion that the subject cannot possibly be of much utility in the real world. However, as this chapter demonstrates, knowing basic mathematical calculations can be an invaluable skill to add to your arsenal.

Math is an indispensable tool for our everyday endeavors. Furthermore, in contrast to the widely accepted notion of math as an abstract subject, practical math permeates across different spheres of our lives. This chapter will dispel that sense of otherworldliness and put math right where it actually belongs: in the midst of our worldly affairs.

This is not a simple matter of math appreciation. Its practical application brings benefit in our everyday lives. With calculation skills at your disposal, you'll worry less about a lot of different concerns. For one, knowing basic calculations will help answer questions you may have asked in one way or another.

These questions may have to do with your utility bills, that bread you've been trying to bake but failed at before, those discounts at the grocery store that sound too good to be true, or perhaps something about your daily calorie count. More importantly, what you will gain is the ability to understand what goes on and what goes where in our affairs, as reflected by numbers—knowledge that would remain obscure to us if we go on irrationally disliking math.

Once again, this goes beyond a lesson on math appreciation. Rather, you will be equipped with the practical mathematical knowledge we all need. Soon enough, you will inevitably realize the myriad ways you can apply math beyond the classroom.

To start off, listed below are just some of the countless ways math can be used in our daily lives:

- Recipes call for measurement units like ounces, cups, and teaspoons. Just getting one wrong could ruin a dish, and probably one's appetite for that matter.

- Decorators need to know that the dimensions of their furnishings and rugs will match the area of your rooms, making it beneficial to be familiar with area, length, breadth, etc. Nothing could be more annoying than buying the wrong fixture and going back and forth to the store just because you chose the wrong size. This is not to mention the additional expenses that could follow.

- When you travel by road, math comes along for the ride. For example, calculating fuel usage is crucial to long-distance travel. Without knowing how much mileage your car has and the fuel you'll need for your journey, you might find yourself stranded or spending too much on gas on the road. You might also have to account for unforeseen detours, road closures, and so on. Furthermore, you'll need to use math for other parts of your trip, like paying for tolls, counting exit numbers, checking tire pressure, etc.

- Math also has a number of applications when it comes to health and wellness. When setting an alarm or hitting snooze, you might want to calculate how much more time you can afford to rest for. If you're on a diet, calculations make counting calories almost effortless. This makes meal planning all the more efficient. Those on medication need to understand different dosages in units such as grams or milliliters.

- Air travelers need to calculate departure times and arrival schedules. We all know that missing a flight can be a nightmare. Calculating your estimated time of arrival in the airport in advance could lessen that risk. It can also help you organize your schedule with practical knowledge of time zones.

- Each time you calculate the price per unit after sales tax or VAT, weigh produce, or incorporate discounts to estimate the final purchase price, you're utilizing math in your shopping experience. If you aren't doing this yet, just imagine how dramatically your financial life can improve when you gain understanding of how these concepts work mathematically.

- If you are planning to pursue an entrepreneurial endeavor, it is inevitable that you'll have to deal with math. It is an indispensable tool starting from the day you decide how much you'll invest, how you will spend it, to paying the taxes, wages, and bills, right down to figuring out how much you have profited. Needless to say, without math skills you will be pretty much blind to the workings of your business. And that blindness is a one-way ride toward bankruptcy.

While these are but a few examples, different spheres of life call for different types of calculations, and this chapter divides mathematical concepts based on why and how math might make your life simpler in particular areas such as shopping, homemaking, school, etc. Math's significance to these daily affairs will be elaborated with the help of some useful math hacks. This approach is particularly useful in driving this chapter's point home.

Math in Shopping

One of the big areas where math is heavily involved in our routine lives is shopping. Regardless of whether you step out to restock your groceries, purchase new clothes, or get a hold of the newest iPhone, you'll find yourself needing mental math for two main reasons: estimating taxes and discounts.

Unlike in some other countries, the price of any given product in the US is not listed with the tax included. This means that you won't know the final purchase price of a product until you reach the cashier. You could be caught off-guard once the tax percentage gets added to the final price. People with a fixed budget could run into trouble. You will be spared from that difficulty if you know how to perform some basic calculations. They will not only help you avoid untoward surprises at the counter, but also allow you to make smart financial decisions as you shop. This includes when you can factor in discounts on particular products to have a better estimate of how much money you're going to spend.

Moreover, when we are shopping, we are usually in the midst of a bustling crowd busily moving around among aisles of shelves. Here, the cumbersome business of pulling out your smartphone and getting into your calculator app each and every time you need to check on prices is just one of the things you have to do. Parents are watching the kids that they bring along with them. Others are carrying heavy grocery bags, pushing carts, and having to hold the product in their hands for a closer inspection. Just imagine the efficiency mental calculations can offer to make your shopping experience less stressful.

Listed below are some easy tips and tricks that can help you calculate taxes or discounts on the go. Make your shopping more enjoyable with the help of these. But not only that, get better at managing finances with improved efficiency.

1) Estimating sales tax

State sales tax in the US is generally listed at approximately 8%, but since this makes calculations more complex, assuming 10% makes things easier without straying too far. A quick way to subtract 10% off an item's purchase price is to simply move the decimal point one place to the left. For example, if you buy a $70.00 item at the hardware store, the tax will be approximately $7.00. Simply add the two numbers (70 + 7 = $77) to obtain the approximate purchase price.

2) Estimating VAT

To calculate VAT, follow the same approach as you would to calculate sales tax: determine 10% by moving the decimal one place to the left. Multiply this number by 2, since VAT tends to hover at 20%. If an item costs $60.00, the sales tax is $6.00, while the VAT becomes $12.00.

3) Calculating a discount

Discounts are usually listed in multiples of either five or ten. Knowing how to calculate discounts proves to be beneficial when shopping, allowing you to mentally estimate the cost of products without having to rely on a calculator. Let's calculate a range of different discounts on a principal of $168.75 for the purpose of demonstration. The general guideline to follow is to calculate up to the nearest multiple of ten (40 if discount is 35%) and use some addition or subtraction for a more accurate estimate.

a. Calculating 25% off

You have two options at your disposal to mentally calculate this:

- 25% is one-fourth of 100%, so we can divide the principal by 4.
- We can use estimates based on two calculations of 10% and one of 5%.

Option one:

Round off $168.75 to 170 and then use strategic division to divide this by 4. This entails first dividing 170 by 2 (= 85), and then dividing 85 by 2 (= 42.50).

If this seems difficult, split the principal amount into two parts and divide each part by 2. For example, 170 can be written as "160 + 10." To obtain the answer, divide both by two and add them together. So 160/2 + 10/2 = 80 + 5, which is 85. Similarly, split 85 into "80 + 5" and divide both by 2 and add the numbers to yield 42.50. Either way, subtract the final number from your principal (170 - 42.50) to arrive at approximately $127.50.

Option two:

For this, find 10% of 170.0 by simply shifting the decimal one place to the left. This gives you 17. To find 5%, divide the number derived from your earlier calculation (17) by 2 to get 8.5. Since the discount is 25%, double the number you obtained from calculating 10% (17 x 2 = 34) and add the value from 5% (34 + 8.5) to yield $42.50.

b) Calculating 30% off

30% is significantly more straightforward since it is a direct multiple of 10. We've already calculated the value of 10% off on 170, which is 17. Simply multiply this number by 3, or add three 17s together by first adding two 17s, and then adding 17 to your answer for easier calculation. 17 + 17 = 34, and 34 + 17 = 51.

51 subtracted from 170 is 119. To simplify this further, reconfigure 51 as "50 + 1" and subtract both figures from 170, which first yields 120 (170 - 50) and then 119 (120 - 1).

c) Calculating 50% off

50% implies half the price, meaning that we only need to divide the principal by 2. 170 divided by 2 = 85, which is both the discount and purchase price after accounting for the discount.

d) Percentage Calculation Tricks

This trick helps you calculate a percentage of any amount with ease. For example, if you need to derive the value of 75% of 20, simply multiply the two numbers together to get 1500.00. Now, shift the decimal two places to the left to get 15, which is the correct answer. This is yet another way to calculate discounts.

a) Calculating percentages

To calculate the percentage of a number that isn't a multiple of ten, simply estimate 1% of that number first and then multiply it.

For example, if you need to calculate 3% of 528, first calculate 1% of it, which can be estimated by moving the decimal two places to the left. This gives us 5.28. Now multiply this figure with the percentage value (3 in this case) to get 15.84.

b) Calculate percentages backward

Often, you'll be forced to calculate with obtuse numbers that complicate estimation. One way to get around this is to remember that x% of y = y% of x. For example, 68% of 25 = 25% of 68 = 68/4 = 17.

This method can simplify many calculations once you've memorized the percentages that equal basic fractions:

10% = 1/10

12.5% = 1/8

16.666...% = 1/6

20% = 1/5

25% = 1/4

33.333...% = 1/3

50% = 1/2

66.666...% = 2/3

75% = 3/4

c) The 10% Trick

To calculate 10% of any given number, move the decimal point one position toward the left. Here are some examples:

10% of 35 = 3.5

10% of 122 = 12.2

10% of 50 = 5

10% of 1 = 0.1

Note the decimal point is always immediately after the one's digit place, even if it isn't explicitly stated.

Suppose we are calculating 10% of 250. It is advisable to begin by rewriting 10% as 10/100 and multiplying by 250. The 10/100 can be reduced by eliminating factors of 10. Another easy way to remember this is to simply cancel equal numbers of zeros in the numerator and denominator. This gives us 1/10 multiplied by 250, which is 250/10. Eliminate the common zero to get 25.

d) Calculating 10% off made simpler

First, subtract 10% from 168.75 by shifting the decimal one place to the left. 10% of 168.75 = 16.875. Round this off to the nearest penny to obtain 16.88.

Since it is 10% off, subtract 16.88 from 168.75. An estimate will suit our purposes so round off 168.75 and 16.88 to the nearest dollar before subtraction. This gives us 169 − 17 = $152. Had we taken the exact values, our answer would only be 13 cents more. $152 thus gives us a sufficiently accurate estimate.

Math at Home

Of course, after shopping, you will be taking all those groceries back home—the second area of our focus. More than what some of us might accept, there is no other place where we need math skills more than the comfort of our own homes. It is one of the fundamental skills that is needed to keep the household running smoothly. This applies first and foremost with budgeting. We also need math for repairing things, installing fixtures, finding the most cost-effective appliances and furnishing the home. Getting the right measurements and arriving at the correct calculations can make or break your budget.

Imagine a scenario where you need to install new carpeting for the living room or sod for your lawn. Different rooms require different sizes of carpets, while lawns aren't always evenly constructed. In both of these cases, knowing how to calculate the area of a room or lawn will go a long way in creating a reliable budget estimate. It also saves you the time and resources spent on hiring someone to make the calculations for you.

Now imagine another scenario, this time in your kitchen. You want to do a complete makeover. Hence, you need to remodel your kitchen and replace your current utensils with new ones. This, of course, will lead to several questions, all of which require some mathematical knowhow. Which containers, measuring cups, bottles, etc. do you need to cook and store your food? What are the right measurements for constructing the new kitchen top? How much money will be needed to put all this together given the space the kitchen has? To answer these questions, you'll need to turn on your knowledge of volumes and areas and how to calculate them.

This section focuses on the building matters inside the home. This is all about how to calculate both area and volume—some of the basic maths involved in renovating or constructing exteriors and interiors. Also included are some neat measurement tricks when you find yourself in a situation where you are missing the measuring tape or ruler.

1) Calculating Area

For this, you'll need values for the length and width of the area you wish to calculate. These can be obtained using a tape or scale of any kind. Simply multiply the two figures together regardless of unit to obtain the area.

area = length × width

2) Calculating Volume

To calculate volume, follow the same procedure as calculating area but with the added dimension of height. After multiplying length and width, multiply the value of height by your answer in accordance with the formula given below.

volume = length × width × height

3) Using Your Body to Estimate Length

Body parts were once a common way to measure objects. In the absence of tapes, rulers, or other devices, they can still be useful to obtain relative estimates. Some ways to use your body for calculations are:

a) Your hand: The width of your palm is approximately 4 inches (10 centimeters).

b) Your foot: The average foot is around 12 inches long.

c) Your forearm from elbow to fingertip: Your forearm is about 1.5 feet (46 centimeters).

d) From nose to fingertip: The distance between your nose and your fingertip when your arm is extended is about a yard (36 inches).

e) The distance of one full stride: Called a pace, this measure amounts to 58 inches, narrowly shy of 6 feet.

Though these are general guidelines, it might be useful to note the measurements of your body parts for more accurate calculations.

Math at School

Math can be enough of a chore as an academic subject all on its own. Nonetheless, there are more math-related things to deal with in school other than attending classes and taking difficult quizzes and tests. We are not necessarily talking about having to implement calculus, or trigonometry for that matter. What we are discussing has more to do with one's grades and academic standing. This adds another proof that math finds a way to permeate every sphere of life.

Essential applications of math in school beyond the class subject include a range of calculations for a student to gauge how she or he is doing academically. From calculating your GPA, to setting up desired targets for your exam scores, these computations are often not straightforward through a phone calculator. Given how simple they are, you likely won't need one anyway once you've grasped the logic behind these concepts. This section will teach you how to calculate your GPA, as well as find balanced averages to help you at school.

1) Calculating GPA

First, convert the grade to numbers using the following scale:

Letter Grade	Number Value
A	4
B	3
C	2

D	1
F	0

Say you're taking four courses and your grades are A, A, C, and D. The numeric equivalents are 4, 4, 2, and 1.

Second, add these numbers together.

Due to the low number of classes taken by students in a single semester or quarter, the addition calculation is fairly basic. In the example, the total is 11. However, the task becomes more challenging while calculating GPAs for a larger number of classes.

Divide the result of your addition by the number of courses considered. In this example, divide by 4. The result is a number greater than 2 and less than 3. To be more specific, it's 2 with a remainder of 3, which amounts to 0.75. Your GPA is 2.75, or about a C+.

2) Finding a Balanced Average

Consider three exam grades:

Exam 1: 80
Exam 2: 99
Exam 3: 92

If you wanted to score an average of 91 in the class overall, how many marks do you need in your fourth and final exam to reach your goal? Instead of pulling out your calculator and solving through a normal average equation, you can estimate this within seconds using mental math.

Take how far each individual grade is off from your target grade and then add the values together.

$(80 - 91) + (99 - 91) + (92 - 91) = -2$

This means that you are 2 points off from making your goal average. This implies that you need 93 in your final exam to score an overall average of 91.

Math and Food

Math and food are closely related. This applies whether you are cooking at home or eating at your favorite restaurant. Shopping for ingredients, measuring them, getting the right temperature for your oven and calculating the bill given by the waiter invariably involves numbers. From the price of fruits or vegetables to the cost of items on a menu and the tip you intend to leave your server, minor calculations abound when it comes to food.

These calculations involve a wide variety of concepts and units, different when you are cooking than when you are eating out. In the kitchen you'll have to deal with the teaspoons, grams, and temperature in Fahrenheit among many other measurements. Get one wrong and you're in a disaster. While in the restaurant, even the tip can be carefully considered before handing out the tab.

These calculations can become more complicated than some of the earlier ones listed in this chapter, and many of the situations mentioned need a quick decision. But they don't have to be sources of suffering. There are a couple of everyday math tips that will help you become a good cook or a generous customer. This section provides you with some easy ways to make food-related calculations simple enough to do it all in your head.

1) Calculating Restaurant Tips

Besides shopping, eating out at restaurants is another area where knowing basic calculations prove to be of great value. Using the trick described below, we can calculate common tip percentages of 10%, 15% and 20% mentally.

a. Calculate a Tip

Most restaurants in the US recommend that you leave a tip for your waiter. Common tips range anywhere from 10 to 25%. Let's assume you want to add 15% to your bill as a tip while processing the calculation mentally. Here's how to perform it:

For a $25 bill, you can calculate an additional 15% as follows.

(10% of $25) + (5% of $25) = 2.5 + 1.25 = 3.75

Here, we split the 15% into 10%+5% and added both percentages to our bill. The values thus derived are again added to arrive at the final amount.

If this method appears to be confusing, you can use the percentage tricks from above and calculate the sum as follows:

2.5 x 1.5 = 3.75

An Alternative Method

For an unspecified tip percentage, simply move the decimal one place to the left in order to get 10% of your bill amount. Then either add half of what you obtained to get 15% or double it for 20%.

For example, if the bill is $43.21, then 4.32 is 10%. Half of 4.32 is 2.16 so if you want 15% just add that to 4.32. This gives you 4.32 + 2.16 = $6.48.

Getting 20% is even easier because you simply need to double the 10% value. 4.32 x 2 = 8.64. Thus, if you're feeling generous, $8.64 would constitute a 20% tip.

2) Calculate the Annual Cost of Your Coffee

For those of us that spend on a morning cup of coffee on our way to work, estimating exactly how much you spend over a year can be tricky given the need to account for off days, etc. With the following trick, you'll be able to make smart financial decisions regarding this minor but constant expense.

If your morning coffee costs $4, then multiply it by the number of times a week you purchase it. Let's assume 5, which means it costs us $20 a week. Add two zeros to the end: $2000. Simply divide that number by 2 and you have a rough yearly cost estimation. That $4 cup of coffee is costing you approximately $1000 a year.

3) Celsius to Fahrenheit Conversion for Recipes

Cooking and baking can require knowing a wide range of mathematical calculations since cookbooks and recipes often use different units for measurement. Knowing how to manipulate fractions, ratios, decimals, etc., are also skills that prove highly beneficial here. One such important calculation is the Celsius to Fahrenheit conversion.

For example, a recipe states that the oven must be set at 220°C, but yours is labeled in Fahrenheit. To convert from Celsius to Fahrenheit in this recipe, follow the following formula:

°C x 9/5 + 32 = °F

220 x 9/5 + 32 = °F
396 + 32 = 428°F

To roughly convert from Celsius to Fahrenheit, multiply by 2 and add 30. To calculate from Fahrenheit to Celsius, subtract 30 and divide by 2. For more precise conversions from C to F, multiply by 1.8 and add 32.

The order is crucial: The addition/subtraction is always closer to the Fahrenheit side of the equation. If you forget the order, remember that 32°F = 0°C, so you can test your formula against that.

Miscellaneous Math Concepts and Their Applications

The mathematical concepts listed in this section might not adhere to any particular category, but knowing them will make mental math and applying them in the previously listed areas simpler and more efficient. As will be described, they also have their own unique applications in cases like calculating yearly or hourly wages, determining adequate ratios for asset allocation, and so on.

1) Convert Miles and Kilometers

To convert miles to kilometers, you can arrive at a fairly accurate estimate by adding 60% to the number of miles. To simply things further, first add 50% followed by adding 10% individually to the principal. 50% implies half, which means you must divide the number of miles by 2, while 10% can be accounted for by multiplying it by 0.1.

For example, 60 miles in km. would be the following: 60/2 = 30 and 60 x 0.1 = 6. Now, add the two values you get, 30 + 6 = 36. Add this to 60 to get 96 km.

To obtain kilometers from miles, subtract 40%. You can do this by first subtracting 50% and then adding 10%. For example, assuming 350 km., first divide it by 2 (350/2 = 175). Now derive 10% of 350.0 by shifting the decimal one place to the left, giving you 35. Subtract the first value (175) and add the second (35). The estimate is thus 210.

Note: Keep in mind that these are vague estimates. The margin for error increases with bigger numbers.

Takeaways

The lack of obvious practical applications is at the heart of disinterest in studying and excelling at math for many who are struggling at the subject. Due to the way we are taught the subject in school, most of us fail to see how we can find x outside the problems listed in our textbooks. Yet math pervades almost every sphere of our practical life in unique and wondrous ways. If we want to cook something, we need math to measure and use the right amount of ingredients.

If we wish to manage our finances efficiently, especially when it involves accounting for the value of fluctuating stocks and the income lost to taxes, we need several different mathematical operations to do so. Even if we just want to decide how much to tip the waiter at a restaurant we visit, we need to be familiar with concepts like percentages. As such, math is practically unavoidable in our daily lives, so it pays to be familiar with at least its most basic concepts.

It is true that we always have the option of relying on the internet or calculators to do our math for us, but no tool can help us if we don't know the procedure for calculating whatever it is we need to find out. Calculators don't input the numbers and operations by themselves; it is we who need to provide them with that data. Yet once we discover how simple it is to perform most of the operations we need in our daily lives, the need for calculators disappears altogether.

There are several mental math tricks which can help you deduce answers in a matter of seconds for a wide variety of applications. Not only will these tricks make you appear intelligent in the company of your peers, being able to do them fills you with a sense of achievement unlike anything else.

Chapter 3. Calculations

The previous chapter highlighted some basic mathematical operations based on certain specific areas of life where they prove especially handy. However, there are still many others of these operations that are more generally useful in diverse situations. You might have to deal with complex percentages as part of your income tax return, or multiplication for your stock options, to give a few examples.

Sometimes, these different situations require the same approaches or methods. We just have to figure out when and where to use them properly. After all, the abstract nature of mathematics, when thinking about it and learning from the history of its development, is not really because the subject is detached from the world. It is rather because most, if not all, of the mathematical forms postulated by mathematicians are the generalized terms extracted and refined from observing and measuring the world. Given that, math can predict and quantify almost all known natural and human-related phenomenon.

As such, this chapter looks into crucial mathematical operations that everyone must be able to perform should we ever need to utilize them. When talking about this crucial everyday math, we are most likely referring to arithmetic. This includes division, multiplication, dealing with fractions, percentages, and many others. Of course, after all our talk about math being so hard, we still know how basic arithmetic works. It is the task of dealing with large figures or inexact numbers that we will definitely find problematic.

Given that, we're not simply talking about learning these various computational methods because, essentially, we already know most of them. We will survive with a calculator or even just a pen and piece of paper. But why just end there? This chapter will teach you mental math hacks when you need answers right away. Also included are methods that will help everyone deal with those unruly decimals and fractions. It tackles various methods to choose from depending on your preference, so you can pick approaches that feel the most comfortable to you.

Mentally multiplying large numbers

Say you want to multiply 96 and 97. Subtract both numbers individually from 100 (100 - 96) and (100 - 97) to get 3 and 4.

Add the two numbers you obtain. 3 + 4 = 7.

Whatever sum you derive, subtract that from 100 as well. 100 – 7 = 93. 9 and 3 are the first two digits of your answer.

Then, multiply the two numbers you obtained and use them as for the tens and units digit places in your answer. Thus, 3 x 4 = 12, and the answer is 9312.

Adding and subtracting fractions using the Butterfly Method

If you can recall your lessons on dealing with fractions in your school days, we know that we can't just simply add or subtract fractions that have different denominators (i.e. the number underneath a fractional number). We have to do something that will make these fractions in question share a common denominator before proceeding to the problem.

We can save our time doing this by simply drawing a butterfly over the two fractions side by side. This is a visual guide that will direct us to understanding and accomplishing the operation. Here's how to add or subtract fractions with the butterfly technique:

1. Write the fractions side-by-side as usual and draw two ovals along the diagonals, encapsulating the numerator of one fraction and the denominator of the other. Then, draw an antenna in the form of a "C" on each "wing."

2. The ovals represent the numbers you need to multiply together. Do so and note the product in the antenna for each wing.

3. Connect the bottom halves of the wings with a loop and multiply the connected denominators. Note the product inside this loop. To remember this step intuitively, imagine it as adding a body to your butterfly. This number is your final denominator.

4. Add or subtract the numbers noted in the antennae in accordance with the operation demanded by the question. This is your final numerator.

5. If necessary, reduce or simplify the result.

Reverse-Zorro Method

The reverse or "backwards" Zorro approach makes finding fractions of a larger number a breeze. The method is called Reverse-Zorro because the flow of the calculation is like writing a mirror image of the letter "Z"—something that the eponymous fictional swordsman usually does, except in the right direction.

We could find this technique useful in situations where we need to buy things that are sold and priced by units of measures like kilograms or liters. Imagine coffee beans or rice that will sometimes not be sold in packs. We wouldn't always buy these by exact one, two, or so on pounds or kilos. Sometimes all we need is half or a quarter of it. The reverse-Zorro method will give you the right price in an instant for this situation.

Assume you need to find what 3/4ths of 24 is. Write the numbers as you normally would, and trace a line to connect the denominator to 24. Divide the denominator by the number assigned to you. In this case, 24 divided by 4 is 6. Then, connect your number with the numerator. Multiply your numerator by the number you derived from division. Finally, trace the last line of the backwards z to note your answer (6 x 3 = 18).

<u>Memorize simple arithmetic</u>

Learning about math tricks doesn't mean we're excused from doing straightforward arithmetical computations or skipping altogether the conceptual part. We will still have to tackle certain concepts because they are at the core of these techniques. Math will become so much easier once we figure how things work on a conceptual level. Therefore, it is important to familiarize yourself with basic calculations involving single and double-digit numbers to aid you in your calculations.

However, it helps to not take the title of this section at face value. In other words, memorizing here doesn't imply that you have to memorize each and every value in the multiplication table or something similar to that. What you need to always keep in mind is how the relationship of numbers and operators work. They have certain patterns, and we can use that to our advantage. Having that understanding will make learning and appreciating these math hacks way easier. For example, knowing the multiples of some numbers will help you deduce those of bigger numbers, thus breaking down a math problem into manageable chunks.

Below are some of the patterns that will be useful in making calculations easier for us. Technically, they are also math hacks as well. What are these tricks anyway, but the patterns of number relationships. They may seem very tough at first, but once you get the gist of them, the details will smoothly follow after.

Find a square number slightly bigger than the biggest one you know

If you recognize the square—meaning the product of a number when multiplied to itself—of a whole number, you can easily find the square of the next whole number. To obtain this, add the first square, the first root number, and the second root number using this equation: $x^2 + x + (x + 1) = (x + 1)^2$.

For example, you know that 10 x 10 is 100. So 11^2 = 100 + 10 + 11, or 121. 12^2 = 121 + 11 + 12 = 144, and 13^2 = 144 + 12 + 13 = 169. And so on.

Obtaining the square of a two-digit number

Say you need to square 46. First round it off to the nearest multiple of 10 (here by adding 4). Then add or subtract the same number (4) to obtain a second number. In this example, you'll have 50 and 42. Then, multiply those two numbers and add the square of the number you used to round off (in this case 4^2). So $46^2 = (50 \times 42) + 4^2 = 2,100 + 16 = 2,116$.

Multiplying 50 and 42 in your mind can be a challenging task, but a way to simplify this is to take a number and multiply it by one of them while dividing it by the other. Using the same example, you can multiply 2 by 50 to get 100, and divide 42 by 2 to obtain 100 x 21, which is much simpler than 50 x 42. Combining mental math tricks in this manner makes the process much more efficient.

Divisibility tests

How can we say that a number is divisible by another without leaving behind a remainder? Numbers hold certain characteristics that give away the answer to the question. For each one-digit number used to divide another larger number, there are corresponding tests to determine whether the latter will leave no remainder.

To illustrate, a number is divisible by 2 if it ends in an even number (i.e. 2, 4, 6, 8) or by zero. A number is divisible by 3 if the sum of all the digits is divisible by 3. For example, 124 is not divisible by 3 because 1 + 2 + 4 = 7, and dividing 7 by 3 will leave behind a remainder. While 123 is divisible by 3 because 1 + 2 + 3 = 6, and 6 is perfectly divisible by 3. A number is divisible by 5 if it ends with either 5 or 0 and divisible by 10 if it ends with 0.

Listed below are some more divisibility tests.

Divisibility by 4

To see if a number is divisible by 4 just note the last two digits. If they are divisible by 4, then the entire number is divisible by 4 as well. So 23746316 will be divisible by 4 because 16 is divisible by 4.

Divisibility by 6

To check if a number is divisible by 6, you need to combine two divisibility rules (twos and threes).

If a number is divisible by both 2 and 3, then it is also divisible by 6. We've already illustrated the test for divisibility by 3, but to restate the test for 2, all even numbers are divisible by 2.

Divisibility by 7

Determining if a number is divisible by 7 involves, first, taking its last digit and then multiplying it by 2. Subtract the result from the remaining digits of the number. If their difference is divisible by 7 then the number is as well. Take note that the steps above may have to be repeated several times, especially when the number is big.

For example, we need to know if 2415 is divisible by 7. Take 5, the last digit, and multiply it by 2, which is 10. Subtract 10 from 241, which results in 231. The number is still quite big to conclude anything, so we have to repeat the process again. Now take 1, the last digit of the previous result, and multiply by 2. Now, 23 minus 2 is 21, which is 3 x 7. Hence, we can conclude that 2415 is divisible by 7.

Divisibility by 8

To see if a number is divisible by 8, observe the last three digits. If they are divisible by 8, then the number is divisible by 8. For example, 3423024 is divisible by 8 because 024/8 = 3, which means that it's perfectly divisible by 8.

Decimal representations

How would certain fractions look in decimal form? We can get a decimal form of a fraction by dividing its numerator by its denominator. Now fractions with certain denominators display a common pattern of how their decimal counterparts will appear. There are easy techniques we can use to figure this out for certain denominators, and they are listed below.

11ths

To represent a fraction with 11 as its denominator in decimals, simply multiply the numerator by 9, and infinitely recur the number you obtain after the decimal point. For example, 2/11 in decimals is 2 x 9 = 18, which is denoted as 0.18181818...

9ths

To represent a fraction with 9 in its denominator as a decimal number, simply repeat the numerator ad infinitum. For example, 2/9 is simply 0.22222...

Mentally adding numbers

To simplify addition in your head, always break down larger numbers to multiples of

10 and add them together till you're left with the units digits. For example, to add 376 + 581, first add 300 + 500 to get 800. Now add on 70 + 80, which is 150. This brings the total to 950. Then add 6 + 1 to get 7, bringing your final tally to 957. Break the addition down into smaller parts from left to right.

Normally we first add the units digit places, carry over the numbers and proceed from right to left. However, our brains are more adept at recognizing and analyzing numbers when read from left to right, a fact this technique exploits to make addition easier. Furthermore, this method is especially useful if you only want to derive an approximate answer, such as the range of order of magnitude the answer lies in.

Mentally subtracting numbers

For mental subtraction, the process is similar to the one utilized for addition. Proceed from left to right, but with one caveat that wasn't included before (hint: it involves rounding). Let's say you wish to subtract 632 – 487. First, add 3 in order to round off 487 to the nearest 10, giving you 490. Rewriting the sum as 632 – 490 makes the operation easier. 632 – 400 is 232. Now subtract 90 to get 142 (it's 10 more than subtracting 100). Just remember to add the three you initially used to round off the number to obtain 145.

Subtracting from 1,000

The basic rule to subtract any large number from 1,000 is this. Subtract each digit of the number (except the last) by 9. For the last digit, subtract 10 by it. Take each individual number obtained and combine them in the same order to obtain the right answer.

For example, if you have to subtract 556 from 1,000:

Step 1: Subtract 5 from 9 = 4

Step 2: Subtract 5 from 9 = 4

Step 3: Subtract 6 from 10 = 4

The answer is 444.

Squares are your friends

Here is an example to illustrate this heading. Let's assume for a moment that we don't know the answer to 10 x 4. The first step is to discover the average number between these two numbers, which is 7 (i.e. 10 – 3 = 7, and 4 + 3 = 7). Next, determine the square of 7, which is 49. We now have a number that's close to the answer, but not close enough. To get the correct answer, we need to square the difference between the averages (in this case 3), providing us with 9. The last step is simple subtraction, 49 – 9 = 40, to yield the correct answer.

Though this technique is ineffective for small calculations, it is a boon for larger ones. Take 15 x 11 for example. Once again, we have to find the average number between these two, which is 13. The square of 13 is 169. The square of the difference in the average (2) is 4. Finally, 169 − 4 = 165, the correct answer.

When performing mental math, particularly with large numbers, it's often beneficial to produce an informed estimate without worrying about obtaining the precise answer. Use the various rules of mental math to simplify the numbers you're presented with. For instance, computing the problem 5 x (14 + 43) is a daunting task by itself, but it can be broken down into three fairly manageable calculations. In accordance with the order of operations, this problem can be rephrased as (5 x 14) + (5 x 40) + (5 x 3) = 285.

Squaring numbers that end in 5

To square any double-digit number that ends in 5, simply multiply the first two digits of the number together and add 25 as the next two digits. For example, 45^2 is 4 x 5 = 20. Take 20 and add 25 as digits at the end to obtain 2025.

Approximating a square root

To approximate a square root, perform the following steps. First, find the nearest perfect square lower than your given number. Add these numbers together. Now divide your result with the square root of the lower perfect square. Then divide this result further by 2.

Here is an example for demonstration. Assume you have to approximate the square root of 31. The next lowest perfect square is 25. Add 31 and 25 to obtain 56. Now divide by the square root of 25, which is 5. 56/5 = 11.2. Divide this result by 2 to get 5.6.

Binomial Theorem for squaring

Use the binomial theorem $(a + b)^2 = a^2 + 2ab + b^2$ to square large numbers. For example, 55^2 can be rewritten as $(50 + 5)^2$. This means that 50 x 50 + 50 x 5 x 2 + 5 x 5 = 2500 + 500 + 25 = 3025.

Scientific notation for huge numbers

When calculating large numbers in your head, remember that you can convert them into scientific notation first. What's 44 billion divided by 400,000? A simple way to deal with this is to convert 4 billion to 10^9, and 400,000 to 10^5. We can now express this as 44/4 and $10^9/10^5$. The rule for dividing exponents requires us to subtract them (easy!), so we get $11 \times 10^{(9-5)} = 11 \times 10^4 = 110,000$.

Handy multiplication tricks

Multiplication can be made much simpler by remembering some tricks to make calculations more efficient. One of the more obvious rules is that any number that's multiplied by 10 only needs to have an additional zero placed at the end.

When multiplying by 12, simply multiply the other number first by 10, then by 2, and add the results together to obtain the final answer. For example, if you need to multiply 4 with 12, first multiply 4 x 10 (= 40), then 4 x 2 (= 8), and add 40 + 8 = 48.

For multiples of 15: First multiply the other number by 10, and take half of the resultant number and add that to the result of x*10. For example, 4 x 15 = 4 x 10 = 40. Add half of 40 (20) to the number derived by the first step (40). 40 + 20 = 60.

There is another handy trick for multiplying by 16. First, multiply the number in question by 10, and then multiply half of the non-16 number by 10. Next, add those two results together along with the number itself to get your final answer. So to calculate 16 x 24, first ascertain 10 x 24 = 240. Then deduce half of 24, which is 12, and multiply by 10, giving you 120. Simply add 240 + 120 + 24 = 384.

Complex multiplication

When multiplying large numbers, observe if one of the numbers is even. If it is, divide the first number in half, and double the second number. This method will help you multiply larger numbers more efficiently. For instance, consider 20 x 120. Divide 20 by 2, which gives 10. Double 120, which equals 240. Then multiply your two answers together. 10 x 240 = 2400. The answer to 20 x 120 is 2,400.

Multiplying 5 times any number

When multiplying the number 5 with an even number, the following is a quick method of discovering the answer. For example, assume you need to calculate 5 x 4.

Step 1: Take the number being multiplied by 5 and halve it. In this case, 4 divided by 2 is 2.

Step 2: Add a zero at the end of this number to find the answer. In this case, the answer is 20.

5 x 4 = 20

When multiplying an odd number by 5, the formula is slightly different. For instance, consider 5 x 3.

Step 1: Subtract one from the number being multiplied by 5. In this instance the number 3 becomes 2.

Step 2: Now halve the number 2 to obtain 1. Make 5 the last digit. The number thus produced is 15, which is the correct answer.

5 x 3 = 15

Multiplying by 9

The following is a simple method that is helpful for multiplying any number by 9. Let's utilize the example of 9 x 3.

Step 1: Subtract 1 from the number that is being multiplied by 9. 3 – 1 = 2. The number 2 is the first digit in the correct answer.

Step 2: Subtract that number from the number 9. 9 – 2 = 7. The number 7 is the second number in the answer to the multiplication problem.

So, 9 x 3 = 27

Multiply by 11

If you want to multiply a number by 11 that doesn't lie between 1 and 9, it can be tricky to perform the calculation in your mind. For example, try to find 11 times 67 in your head—quickly.

Instead of attempting to straightforwardly multiply the two numbers, do this instead. Take the number you wish to multiply by 11 (here 67) and separate the numbers. Then, take the digits, add them together, and place them in between the original number:

6 (6 + 7) 7 = 6 13 7

If your sum is 10 or more, carry the 1 over to 6 while keeping the 3 undisturbed to obtain the final answer of 737.

Multiplying numbers that end in zero

Multiplying numbers that end in zero is fairly straightforward. All you need to do is multiply the other digits and add the cumulative number of zeroes. For instance, consider: 200 x 400

Step 1: Multiply 2 times 4. 2 x 4 = 8

Step 2: Put all four of the zeros after the 8 to obtain 80,000

200 x 400 = 80,000

FOIL method for multiplication

To multiply two numbers together, utilize the FOIL method (first, outer, inner, last). For example, if you had to multiply (25 + 10) with (30 + 4), start with multiplying the first numbers of the binomials (25 x 30). Then, take the numbers on the two extremes and multiply them (25 x 4). Next, take the innermost two numbers and do the same (10 x 30) and finally, take the second number of each binomial and multiply them (10 x 4). Add all these sets together to obtain the final answer. (25 x 30) + (24 x 4) + (10 x 30) + (10 x 4) = 916.

Note: This process is no different from the one used in ordinary multiplication. You can split any two large numbers and multiply them with this method. The FOIL technique simply makes it easier to understand the process while simplifying it simultaneously.

Multiply by rounding

This method is especially suitable if one of your numbers is a multiple of 10. If so, simply round off the other number and multiply the two together. For example, if you have to multiply 18 and 30, just round off 18 to 20, multiply 20 x 30 to get 600 and subtract two 30s to obtain 540.

Mental Math: the skills of calculating fast.

Mental math skills can broadly be divided into three categories:

1) Offensive.

The purpose here is to obtain the result fast.

Example: Compute 47 x 53.

Answer: Take the average of these two numbers, which is 50. This is deduced by adding and subtracting 3 from the respective numbers. Square both these numbers and subtract the results to obtain the correct answer. $50^2 = 2500$, $3^2 = 9$. Therefore, 47 x 53 = 2500 - 9 = 2491.

2) Defensive.

The purpose is to quickly establish the implausibility of a result.

For example, compute 91 x 18. The given answer is 1538.

Answer: This is obviously wrong because 18 is divisible by 9 and so must be the product of 91 x 18. However, 1538 is not divisible by 9 since its digits add up to 1 + 5 + 3 + 8 = 17, which is not divisible by 9. The correct answer is 1638.

3) Entertaining.

The purpose here is to dazzle with any chosen method of obtaining a result as much as through the result itself.

Example: Think of a 3-digit number. Write it in reverse. Subtract the two smaller digits from the largest one. If you're told the first two digits of the answer, one can easily deduce the last digit.

Percentages

Finding the percentage of any given number can be somewhat tricky, but conceptualizing the problem using the right terms simplifies the process. For instance, to deduce what 5% of 235 is, follow this method:

Step 1: Move the decimal point one place to the left for the number you're finding the percentage of. Here, 235 becomes 23.5.

Step 2: Divide the resulting number, 23.5, by the 2. The answer is 11.75. 11.75 is also the answer to 5% of 235.

Switching percentages

Here is a neat trick that is very hard to forget due to its elegant simplicity: x% of y is the same as y% of x. This means that if 2% of 50 is too hard to figure out, you can simply switch the positions of the numbers to get 50% of 2, which will yield you the same answer while being easier to calculate in your head.

Miscellaneous calculation methods

1) Multiplying by 5

If you need to multiply a number by 5, it might be easier to half it and then multiply by 10. For example, 315 x 5 would be 315/2 = 157.5 Now just move the decimal one place to the right to obtain 1575.

2) Dividing Numbers by 5

When dealing with small numbers like 10, dividing by 5 is a simple process. However, when you consider a larger value like 215, it can be hard to calculate quickly. The following trick simplifies the process regardless of the number:

Simply take the number, multiply it by 2, and move the decimal point one place to the left.

215 x 2 = 430 → 43

It's that simple. If you want to divide a number, say 423, which isn't divisible by 5, simply round it off to the nearest multiple of 5 or 10 (420 or 425 in this case) and repeat the same process.

3) Turn Repeating Decimals into Fractions

If you obtain an answer that ends in .63636363, it can be difficult to convert this into fraction form. All you need to do in such cases is to take the recurring part of the decimal, 63, and divide it by a figure of nines with as many digits as the recurring number. In layman's terms:

63/99 = 7/11. If the number was .456456456, divide 456/999.

You likely won't be able to perform this trick in your head, but it is nevertheless a useful skill to know in order to quickly convert recurring decimals into fractions on a regular calculator. 7/11 is far easier to understand than .63636363636363636363....

4) Converting Hourly to Yearly Wage and Vice Versa

Comparing the salaries offered by different employers can be tricky depending on the way they phrase the amount. Say one offers you $60,000 a year, while the other promises $31 an hour. Which is the better paying job? Here is how to find out:

Take your yearly wage and drop the last three digits before dividing the result by two. For example, a $60,000 a year job pays out 60/2 or $30 per hour.

Thus, you would be better off taking the $31 an hour job based on pay. You can also use your hourly wage to calculate yearly wages in a similar manner. $31 times 2 equals 62. After adding three zeros, you get $62,000 a year. Your annual salary is around 2,000 times your hourly rate.

a) Precise Salary Calculations

Your annual salary is your hourly rate, multiplied by the number of hours you work in a week, further multiplied by 52 weeks. Assuming an hourly rate of $8 with 5 hours of work per week, this amounts to 8 x 5= 40. 40 x 52 is $2,080. However, to calculate this mentally, you can round off 52 to 50 to obtain 2,000, which makes for an accurate ballpark figure.

5) Asset Allocation Trick

If you are investing and trying to determine how much of your money to expend on stocks or fixed income returns like bonds, you can use this simple trick and some general guidelines for a reliable estimate.

Subtract your age from 120, and this is the percentage that should be invested in stocks. Thus, if you are 45, then 75% of your entire investment should be in stocks.

6) How to Tell if a Number is Evenly Divisible by Another Number

- All multiples of 2 end in 0, 2, 4, 6, or 8.

- All multiples of 3 have digits that add up to 3, or another multiple of 3.

- Multiples of 4: Take the number formed by the single and tens digits (first two from right to left) and divide it by 2. If you get 2, 4, 6, or 8, the entire number is evenly divisible by 4.

- All multiples of 5 end in 5 or 0.

- Multiples of 6: Run the multiples of 2 test and the multiples of 3 test. If

both are valid, the number is
divisible by 6.

- Multiples of 7: There are a few
  different tests, but they are all harder
  than digging out your phone. This
  one is the easiest:

Double the units digit number and subtract from the number formed by the remaining digits repeatedly. For example, if your number is 1365, take 5 and double it to get 10, then subtract this from 136 to obtain 126. Now, take 6, double it to get 12, and subtract from 12 to get 0. If the chain ends in 0 or a multiple of 7, then the original number is divisible by 7.

- Multiples of 8: Take the number
  formed by the last three digits
  (hundreds, tens, and units) and
  divide by 4, or half it twice. Then run
  the multiples-of-2 test.

- All multiples of 9 have digits that add up to 9 or a multiple of 9.

- All multiples of 10 end in 0.

To test divisibility by a larger number, try to factor it down to single-digit numbers, then run the tests listed above, keeping any repeated factors together. For example, 60 = 2 x 2 x 3 x 5. So all multiples of 60 are also multiples of 2, 4, 3, and 5.

Some multiplication shortcuts

To multiply a large number in your head, try converting it into a smaller one. For example: even numbers, such as 4 or 6, can be broken down into 2 x 2 and 2 x 3 respectively. If you have to multiply a number with either of these, proceed in a step-by-step fashion by multiplying each factor individually.

- Multiply by 5: First multiply by 10, then divide by 2.

- Multiply by 9: Multiply by 10 and subtract the number. For example, to obtain 65 x 9, first multiply 65 by 10 to get 650. Then, subtract your result with the original number (650-65) to get 585.

- Multiply a single-digit number x by 9: The first digit is x-1. The second digit is 9 minus the first digit. So 8 x 9 = 72.

Takeaways

The overwhelming majority of the arithmetic we need to learn for routine tasks such as cooking, tipping, calculating our grades, and managing finances all boils down to becoming competently efficient at the five key operations. These are addition, subtraction, multiplication, division, and percentages.

Expressing numbers in different forms, such as fractions and decimals, also figures into this discussion because, essentially, these are but other ways that we can express percentages.

As we've gotten to know the behavior of the numerical forms through their interaction with these arithmetic operations, it is tempting to assume they are simple enough that there's no need for more extensive study. It might seem like all we need is a little brushing up on the basics, along with some paper or perhaps a calculator. Paradoxically enough, this kind of mindset could coexist with the math aversion mindset mentioned early on.

Nonetheless, as the saying goes, there is more than one way to skin a cat. There are many different ways we can use the five aforementioned concepts to our advantage. Depending on one's preferences and the techniques that come naturally to them, we can choose from several equally valid procedures to solve a problem. In line with this book's goal, we want to become confident enough to do the math necessary for our everyday affairs. But beyond that, we are also aspiring to a level of improvement that will further develop our cognitive capacities. Hence, the approach that fortifies our mental math abilities.

The beauty of mental math is that we can perform every single one of these procedures using our mind alone, without needing pens, papers, or calculators. In many instances, we don't require answers that are accurate to the last decimal digit.

Approximations suffice, and serve our purposes adequately. Regardless of which method you choose to pursue, the secret to achieving the right answer, whether precise or approximate, is in the ability to convert complex calculations into ones that are more easily comprehensible. In other words, we address these problems by breaking them down to manageable portions.

For example, if you need to multiply something by 11, multiply the number by 10 instead and simply add the number to your product. This is but one of the many ways to reduce problems that seem too complicated to solve in our minds into ones that can be simplified in seconds. Having said that, most of the calculations we are confronted with in our daily lives are fairly simple, and can easily be tackled with just five concepts from the world of math.

Chapter 4. Vedic Math

Chapters two and three provided us with many useful mathematical tools that we can use to better navigate the affairs and demands of our everyday lives. The problem, which is no minor matter, is that there are just too many of these tools. It is a sure bet that the average person would barely remember half of these, much less retrieve the knowledge in an instant when the need presents itself. At best, we need a cheat sheet to bring everywhere we go, but this is quite a self-defeating idea when it comes to the goal of empowering one's mental math prowess.

The core of our quandary lies within the unsystematic and decentralized nature of how we learn and even do arithmetic in the conventional Western mathematical paradigm. These characteristics are detrimental if we want the ability to handle complex operations mentally in an instant. For this to even be possible, one must have a deeper understanding of mathematical concepts. More importantly, there should be a central system that will inform our approach to different mathematical situations and requirements.

Enter, Vedic mathematics.

Vedic mathematics is the name given to an ancient system of Indian math which was rediscovered from Hindu scriptures called the Vedas between 1911 and 1918 by Sri Bharati Krishna Tirthaji Maharaja (1884-1960). Sri Bharati Krishna Tirthaji Maharaja was born in March 1884 in the Puri village of the modern state of Orissa. He was highly proficient in subjects like mathematics, science, humanities and particularly excelled at the language of Sanskrit.

He rediscovered the Vedic sutras while practicing meditation in a forest. He claims that he derived sutras/techniques primarily from the "Rig-Veda" over the course of his eight-year-long meditative practice. He also emphasized the role of intuition in deducing these various sutras. In 1957, he wrote an introductory volume of sixteen sutras called "Vedic Mathematics" and planned to write more sutras in a future tome. However, he unfortunately developed cataracts in both of his eyes and passed away in 1960.

Indian mathematics has made several crucial contributions to the discipline of math, without which the subject might not have progressed beyond its infancy. The invention of zero and the concept of decimal notation are a few examples that trace their origin to India. The success of Indian math in shaping the discipline at large establishes Vedic mathematics as the primal source and springboard from which all of modern Western man's scientific and technological achievements have emanated.

The Vedic math system is based upon sixteen main and thirteen sub-sutras, which are formulas that can be applied to various math problems. For example, "Vertically and Crosswise" is an example of a sutra. These formulae essentially describe the process that needs to be followed to obtain the right answer to a given problem. Thus, remembering the sutra is equivalent to remembering the steps of certain types of math problems. There is research to indicate that Vedic math exploits the natural ways in which the brain perceives and analyzes numbers, making deductions simpler and more efficient.

Think of the different sutras as you would conceive of the various tools in a carpenter's tool belt. For example, if you're faced with a loose Phillips head screw, a sutra acts as the screwdriver to tighten the loose end. If something needs to be measured, there is a sutra that acts as a tape measure. If a nail needs to be driven into a board, there is a sutra that acts as a hammer. Similarly, depending on the nature of any given mathematical problem (whether it is arithmetic, algebraic or geometric), there is a corresponding sutra that can be applied to obtain the answer.

Our Western system of math can often appear as a series of disconnected tools that have been combined to form the discipline of math, whereas Vedic math radiates with a beautiful unity of sutras. The general multiplication method, for example, is easily reversed to allow one-line divisions. The simple squaring method can be altered to obtain single line square roots. The unity of sutras in Vedic math makes the process of learning it far more intuitive and interesting compared to other systems of math. It enables you to solve problems one would ordinarily consider large and complex with ease through its coherent and interdependent techniques. Furthermore, Vedic mathematics is not only a sophisticated pedagogic and research tool, but also an introduction to one of the most advanced civilizations that has ever graced the earth.

So how can Vedic mathematics help us get better at doing our everyday calculations?

There are a number of advantages to learning Vedic math, some of which have been hinted at in the previous section. At the most basic, it is both simpler and more interesting than regular Western math. Even basic knowledge of this system helps enrich your understanding of general mathematics by demonstrating the wondrous ways in which different methods and tools are interconnected to form one coherent discipline.

Vedic math is very helpful in performing complex calculations in short amounts of time. In practical terms, this is especially useful for a board or entrance exam that includes math problems. It is a reliable tool whether you are taking an exam in the field of management, banking, engineering, or any other area of knowledge for that matter. These exams tend to have notoriously short time limits per question. Vedic math can help you complete these tests well ahead of time.

Indeed, many math scholars claim that using Vedic math tricks can improve calculation speeds by up to ten to fifteen times compared to the rudimentary methods we generally follow. This is because Vedic math reduces all problems to one-line answers and negates the need for calculators by using simple sutras that are intuitively understandable by anyone and everyone.

Moreover, Vedic math has also been tested for efficiency by computer scientists who ran the sutras through a computer using an algorithm. The findings displayed a positive result.

Vedic math is especially beneficial for children since it helps cultivate an interest in numbers and calculations from an early age. In modern-day India, there are interest groups that push for Vedic math's introduction to the school curriculum. Once Vedic math sparks an interest in children, a sustained practice brings positive effects in terms of cognitive development.

The usage of sutras helps sharpen mental faculties such as memory, creativity, agility, and intelligence, enabling students not just to excel at math, but in other academic areas as well. Given the simplicity and intuitiveness of Vedic math, any child of sufficient age can easily take it up and master it within a short period of time.

Many calculations facilitated by this system can be done purely through mental math and do not require papers or pencils. This helps children view math in a positive light and avoid the anxiety that so many develop at the prospect of performing calculations. Not only does this promote healthier living, it also gives them a better chance of succeeding at life.

Vedic math has been climbing in popularity as more and more people realize the multiplicity of benefits it has to offer for all types of people. From professionals, to children and young adults, everyone can benefit from even a basic introduction to this system of math.

Sutra 1: Ekadhikena Purvena (By one more than the previous one)

This sutra has two primary uses.

First, this sutra helps you quickly square any number ending with 5. The following is an example to illustrate this. Say you want to find the answer for 75^2, or 75 x 75. The answer, 5625, can be divided into two parts, 56 and 25. Remember that the last two digits of the square of any number ending with 5 are always 25. However, the first two digits are the result of 7 (the first digit of the number you want to square) multiplied by a number that is *"one more"* than it (8). 7 x 8 = 56.

Thus, the answer is 5625. Similarly, 85^2 = 7225. This can be derived by taking 8, the first digit of the number to be squared and multiplying it by 9, the number that comes after it. 8 x 9 = 72. Simply add 25 as the last two digits to obtain 7225. So to generalize, in obtaining the square of a two-digit number that ends in 5, place 25 at the end of the result and then multiply the tens digit of the number to be squared by the number plus one.

Second, you can use this sutra to multiply two numbers that have the same first digit, and whose last digits add up to obtain 10. For example, if we multiply 32 and 38, the answer yielded is 1216. Both 32 and 38 start with 3, and the last digits (2 and 8) add up to 10. Thus, we take the first digit (which is common) and multiply it with the number that comes next (4). 4 x 3 = 12. Then multiply the last digits of both numbers, 8 x 2, to obtain 16. Combine the two to get 1216. Similarly, 81 x 89 = 7209. Multiplying the common first digit with the next whole number, 8 x 9, yields 72. Multiplying the last digits, 9 x 1, gives 09. Joining the two thus gives us 7209.

As demonstrated by this sutra, Vedic math makes you memorize one small line that encapsulates an entire process to help you solve different types of math problems. Not only is this technique more efficient, it is simply more interesting than ordinary multiplication.

Sutra 2: Nikhilam Navatashcaramam Dashatah (All from 9 and the last from 10)

This sutra is ideally suited for multiplying numbers close to bases such as 10, 100, 1000, etc. However, you can use it for any two conceivable numbers.

The following is an example that will help demonstrate this sutra. Say we need to multiply 8 and 7.

Apply the sutra "All from 9 and last from 10" to both these numbers, subtracting them by 10 each since we only have one digit in both. This yields -2 and -3. Now note the problem in the format outlined below:

8-2

× 7-3

_____

- Multiply (-2) and (-3) to get 6 and write it down as below.

8-2

× 7-3

_____ 6_

Next, we need to add the numbers diagonal to each other. This implies that 8 is added with (-3) and 7 is added with (-2). Both yield 5, so we only need to add one pair of numbers. Combine the two numbers obtained from this process to get 56, which is the correct answer.

Sutra 3: Urdhva-Tiryagbhyam (Vertically and crosswise)

This sutra will help you multiply any given pair of large numbers without utilizing multiplication tables beyond 5 x 5.

Multiplying numbers close to 10

For numbers close to 10, assume you need to multiply 8 x 7. Ascertain the number that needs to be added to obtain 10 for each numeral. 8 is 2 less than 10, and 7 is 3 below 10. Next, subtract crosswise such that you obtain 8 - 3 (or 7 - 2) to get 5. This is the first digit of the answer. Then, multiply vertically: 2 x 3 to get 6, the last figure of the answer. Thus, the answer is 56.

To generalize the process: (a) subtract both the respective numbers that need to be multiplied by 10; (b) in a crosswise manner, subtract the resulting previous difference of one number from the other number to be multiplied and vice versa—both should give you the tens digit of the answer; and (c), multiply the differences that resulted in the first step—this should give you the ones digit of the answer.

To take another example, let's observe 7 x 6 = 42. 3 and 4 need to be added respectively to make the numbers equal to 10. By cross-subtracting, we obtain 3, the first digit of the answer. Multiplying the deficiencies yields 12. Here, 1 gets carried over to 3, making it 4. Combine 4 and 2 to obtain 42, the correct answer.

Multiplying numbers close to 100

The first is applied for one-digit multiplication of numbers *both* approaching the number ten. This time, the following method illustrates how to use this sutra to multiply numbers close to 100. Assume you want to multiply 88 by 98. Though this calculation appears to be complex, the sutra greatly simplifies the process. Below are the steps you need to follow:

a. Both 88 and 98 are close to 100. 88 is 12 less than 100, and 98 is 2 below 100.

b. Just like with multiplying numbers close to 10, 86 is derived from subtracting crosswise: 88-2 = 86 (or 98 - 12 = 86—you yield the same answer regardless of which pair you subtract). 86 is the first part of our answer.

c. Multiply the deficiencies, 12 x 2, to obtain 24, the second part of our answer. Thus, we obtain 8624.

Multiplying numbers just over 100.

To demonstrate this, let's take the example of 103 x 104 = 10712.

Like before, we learn the method by breaking down the results first. 107 can be rewritten as 103 + 4 (or 104 + 3), and 12 is just 3 x 4. Take the combination of two units-place digits and multiply them together. Add this result to the sum obtained by adding either 103 + 4 or 104 + 3.

Calculating 107 x 106 = 11342 follows a similar process. First, deduce the difference between 107 and 100, and between 106 and 100. This yields 7 and 6. 7 x 6 = 42. These are the last two digits of your answer. For the last step, simply add 107 + 6 or 106 + 7 to get 113, the first part of the correct answer. Combine the two to obtain the final result, 11342.

Using the sutra to add and subtract fractions

Assume two fractions 2/3 and 1/5 need to be added. Cross multiply the numerator of one with the denominator of the other to obtain 2 x 5 = 10 and 1 x 3 = 3. Add the two results, 10 and 3, together to yield 13. This is the numerator of your answer. The denominator can be obtained by simply multiplying the denominators of the two fractions, 5 and 3, to get 15. Thus, the answer is 13/15.

Subtracting fractions follows the same process, but instead of adding the result of cross-multiplication, subtract them to obtain the numerator. Yield the denominator by multiplying as before.

To illustrate, let us subtract the given two fractions. Again, it is 2 x 5 = 10 and 1 x 3 = 3. 10 - 3 = 7. This is your numerator. Just the same, the denominator is 15 because it is the product of the denominators.

Sutra 4: Shunyam Saamyasamuccaye (When the sum is the same that sum is zero)

This sutra is helpful in deriving the missing value of x in a given simple algebraic equation with one variable (i.e. x).

The sutra essentially states that if the terms of the equation have a common element, and the sum of its parts equals 0, the common term can be equated to 0 as well. This is illustrated through the following method:

Example 1: Assume a linear equation, 2x + 4x - 12x + 16x = 0.

Here, the common term in all the elements of the equation is x. According to the sutra, since the equation itself is equated with 0, we can equate the common term, x, with 0 as well. When we do an algebraic operation for these types of equations (i.e. all terms in the equation contain the variable x, and without a constant term which means to be any number without an x term), we will end up having to divide zero by a number, which we all know will always end up resulting to zero.

Example 2: $7(x + 1) = 8(x + 1)$

The objective is to find x. The standard method would demand that we expand both sides and follow a long and complex procedure to obtain an answer that can be derived much more efficiently through the sutra. The common term here is $(x + 1)$, and the equation also equates to zero when one side is transposed to the other. Transposing one side to the other, for those not familiar with how algebra works, means that the equation on the right side can be transferred over to the left as long as you change its sign from positive to negative or vice versa. This works with both numbers and variables such as x. Hence, we can equate x + 1 with 0, to conclude that x = -1.

Sutra 5: Gyarasguna Sutra (One number can be easily multiplied by 11)

This sutra will help you easily multiply any number by 11. This is one of the easiest sutras with a fairly straightforward method of application. Moreover, this is one of the most well-known sutras and perhaps you may have encountered this technique before, in one way or the other. What it essentially does is it converts a multiplication problem into a simple addition one. To demonstrate with an example, assume you want to multiply 44 by 11. Follow the steps given below.

Step 1: Write the non-11 number twice with an addition sign in between the two.

44 + 44

Step 2: Add a zero in the units digit place of either number.

440 + 44

Step 3: Simply add the two numbers together. 440 + 44 = 484. 484 is the correct answer.

It's incredible how simple this sutra makes multiplications involving 11. It can also be used for problems that involve multiples of 11. For example, if you had wanted to multiply 44 by 44, you could rewrite the problem as 44 x 11 x 4—effectively breaking down the problem into manageable factors of 11. Solve the first half of the problem using this sutra, and then simply perform basic multiplication by multiplying your answer by 4.

Sutra 6: Paravartya Yojayet (Transpose and adjust)

This sutra can be used to divide any number with a divisor that is more than 10. This sutra can seem fairly convoluted at first, but it is an invaluable tool to divide large numbers, especially when the dividend is large since the sutra involves splitting it into two parts. Assume you want to divide 1225 by 12. Follow the steps described below.

Step 1: Discard the first digit of the divisor (12) and then transpose the other remaining digit. The transposition of any number, again, is simply that same number with a negative sign.

12   122   5
-2

Write down the dividend beside the divisor, but separate the last digit. As a general rule of thumb, the number of digits you need to separate from the dividend will always be one less than the number of digits in the divisor. So if your divisor has three digits, separate two from the dividend. Here, we have two digits, so we separate just one.

Step 2: Note the transposition of the second digit below the dividend, and bring the first digit of the dividend below the line as shown below.

```
12     122   5
-2     -2
       --------
       1
```

Step 3: Multiply the transposed number with the first digit (which was brought below the line) and add the value of the transposed number without the negative sign. In this case, 1 x - 2 = -2. Add 2 from the transposed number to yield 0. Note whatever your result is below the second digit of the dividend and perform simple addition.

```
 12    122   5
 -2    -20
       --------
       102
```

Step 4: Now multiply the third digit of the dividend (-2) with the transposed number and note the result below the separated digit of the dividend. 2 x -2 = -4. Note -4 below 5 and perform a simple addition.

```
 12    122   5
 -2    -20  -4
       -----  ------
       102   1
```

102 is the quotient, and 1 is the remainder.

Sutra 7: Anurupyena-Sunyamanyat (If one is in a ratio, the other is zero)

This sutra is generally used to resolve simultaneous equations. These two equations, $3x + 4y = 1$ and $4x + 12y = 3$, are such equations. They are simultaneous in a sense that these two separate equations share the common values for both x and y.

If either the two x or y coefficients (the numbers preceding the two variables; this technically means four multiplied by the x value and y multiplied by 12) are in the same ratio as the independent terms (the ones that come after the equals sign; this is also called the *constant* in math speak), then the "other" variable is equal to zero.

For example, in the equations we've described here, the coefficients of the y-term in both cases (4 and 12. 4/12 can be reduced to 1/3) are in the same ratio as the independent terms (1 and 3). This means that the value of x is zero.

The following is another example but with way larger coefficients just to illustrate how the sutra works for the given precondition.

Assume your equations are 175x + 140y = 350 and 350x + 324y = 700.

Step 1: Form ratios of both coefficients of x and y. Here, this will give you 175:350 and 140:324.

Step 2: Reduce the first ratio as far as possible. 175/350 can be reduced to 1/2. Notice if this ratio is the same as that formed by the independent terms.

Step 3: The independent terms form a ratio 350:700, which can be reduced to 1/2. This is the same as the one derived from the x coefficients, which implies that the value of y is 0.

Step 4: Substitute 0 as the value of y and rewrite the equations. Now, they are 175x = 350 and 350x = 700.

Step 5: Divide the coefficient of x with the independent term in both equations. 350/175 and 700/350 equal 2. Therefore x = 2.

Sutra 8: Sankalana-Vyavakalanabhyam (By addition and subtraction)

This is yet another sutra intended to solve simultaneous equations. To use this sutra, the coefficient of one variable in any equation must be the same coefficient of the second variable. So if your equations are $2x + 3y = 5$ and $3x + 2y = 6$, the coefficient of x in the first equation here is the same as that of y in the second equation. Similarly, the coefficient of y in the first equation is the same as the coefficient of x in the second. This means that the sutra can be used to solve these equations. The following steps describe the precise method using the same example.

Step 1: Add both equations together to get $5x + 5y = 11$.

Step 2: Now subtract both of them to obtain $-x + y = -1$.

Step 3: Simply solve these equations simultaneously to yield the value of both variables, which is $x = 8/5$ and $y = 3/5$.

Sutra 9: Puranapuranabyham (By the completion or non-completion)

This is a sutra meant to solve quadratic equations. Quadratic equations have a single variable but also include exponential terms of that variable. This sutra enables you to simplify complex equations involving cubes of variables. Any equation of the form $x^3 + x^2 + x +$ (independent term) can be solved using this method. For the purpose of demonstration, assume you want to simplify $x^3 + 6x^2 + 11x + 6 = 0$.

Step 1: First we need to find a term of the form $x +$ (any independent term) which, when cubed, most closely resembles the quadratic equation we need to simplify. Basically, we need to find a perfect cube that is nearest to the example. To take an example, consider $(x + 1)^3$. We know we can't simply cube the independent term, 1, which will still yield us only 1. However, the independent term in the given equation is 6, so we need a term that yields a number closer to that. Consider now $(x + 2)^3$. When expanded, this becomes $x^3 + 6x^2 + 12x + 8$, which is extremely similar to the equation we've chosen.

Step 2: Subtract the left-hand sides of both equations. This will yield you $(x + 2)$. Add this to both sides of the original equation to obtain $x^3 + 6x^2 + 12x + 8 = x + 2$.

Step 3: Notice that the left side of this equation is the same as the left-hand side of what we derived when expanding $(x + 2)^3$. Replace the left-hand side with this cubed term.

Step 4: We now have the same term on both sides. For easier determination of values, replace x + 2 with y to yield $y^3=y$.

Step 5: From this, we can infer that y must be either 0, -1, or 1. Equate all three of these independent terms with x + 2 and derive the value of x in each case.

Sutra 10: Yaavadunam (Whatever the extent of its deficiency)

Though the translation might appear to be phrased awkwardly, this sutra will help you deduce the square of any number in just three steps. It uses the "*deficiency*," or the amount any given number is lesser than its nearest power of 10 (10, 100, 1000, etc.) to derive the square of that number. This is illustrated with an example below. Assume you want to find the square of 98.

Step 1: Take the nearest power of 10 and subtract 98 from it. In this case, the nearest power is 100. 100 − 98 = 2. 2 is thus the deficiency.

Step 2: Subtract the deficiency from the original number you wanted to square. 98 - 2 = 96. 9 and 6 are the first two digits of your answer.

Step 3: The right side of your answer is the square of the deficiency. 2 x 2 = 4. However, the right side must have as many digits as there are zeros in the nearest power of 10 you've chosen. 100 has two zeros, so we must denote 4 as 04. 9604 is the correct answer.

Sutra 11: Vyashtisamanstih (Part and whole)

This sutra is mainly utilized either in problems relating to probabilities or simultaneous equations. However, in its latter function, it proceeds in a way that is very similar to the Paravartya sutra. Hence, we'll demonstrate its usage through a probability question. Say you have a bag containing 4 apples, 8 mangoes, and 12 bananas. What is the probability of choosing each type of fruit from the bag?

Step 1: Add the values of all items listed. 4 + 8 + 12 = 24.

Step 2: To find the part and whole ratio of any one item with the whole we derived in step 1, simply form a ratio with the whole as the denominator. Thus, the part-whole ratio of apples is 4/24, that of mangoes is 8/24, etc.

Sutra 12: Shesanyankena Charamena (The remainders by the last digit)

This sutra is used for expressing fractions in decimals, and is especially beneficial when dealing with a fraction that might yield a long, recurring decimal value. In other words, the decimal might go on forever, but in a certain repetitive pattern. These kinds of numbers are called *rational numbers* in math speak. For example, assume you want to convert 1/7 into a decimal. Follow the steps described below to obtain the answer:

Step 1: Keep adding zeros to the numerator until it exceeds the denominator. In this case, we only need to add one zero to make the fraction 10/7.

Step 2: Perform the resulting division and note the quotient and remainder. For our example the quotient is 1 and the remainder would be 3.

Step 3: Take the remainder and add a zero to it. This yields 30. Divide this with the original denominator; we will obtain 4 as the quotient and 2 as the remainder.

Step 4: Repeat step 3 until you obtain the original number as the remainder to your division. In this case, you'll need to repeat the step 4 more times. 20/7 yields 2 as quotient and 6 as remainder. 60/7 yields 8 as quotient with 4 as remainder. 40/7 yields 5 as both quotient and remainder. Finally, 50/7 yields 7 as quotient and 1 as remainder. Make a note of all the remainders you've obtained (3, 2, 6, 4, 5, 1).

Step 5: Now, multiply all the remainders thus obtained with the original denominator (7), and take the rightmost digit of all the answers you obtain.

7 x 3 = 21. Note 1.

7 x 2 = 14. Note 4.

7 x 6 = 42. Note 2.

7 x 4 = 28. Note 8.

7 x 5 = 35. Note 5.

7 x 1 = 07. Note 7.

The decimal representation is 0.142857142857. This will go on forever, but the value we've gotten from the process is the repeating value of the decimal number. The reason we stopped at the original numerator in step 4 is because we would've obtained the same set of values if we had proceeded.

Sutra 13: Sopaantyadvayamantyam (The ultimate and twice the penultimate)

This sutra will help you multiply any number with a divisor of two or more digits using the "penultimate" digit of the divisor. To illustrate, assume you want to multiply 132 by 12.

Step 1: Insert a zero at both ends of the dividend. Here, this yields 01320.

Step 2: Take the last digit and add with the result of multiplying the second last digit with "twice the penultimate" digit of the divisor. The equation is thus last digit + (2 x penultimate digit x second-last digit).

Taking the current example, this is 0 + (2 x 1 x 2) = 4.

Step 3: Repeat step 2 until you've reached the last digit. Thus, the next step is to take the second-last digit, and add it with the result of multiplying 2 and the third-last digit. 2 + (2 x 3) = 8. Next, 3 + 2(1) = 5. Lastly, 1+2(0) = 1.

Step 4: The answer comprises all values from bottom to top. Hence, the correct answer is 1584.

Sutra 14: Ekanyunena Purvena (By one less than the previous one)

This sutra is fairly similar to the sutra explained above that has to do with multiplying eleven or factors of it. This one in particular is used to multiply a number with a number that is either 9 or an array of 9s (9, 99, 999, etc.). Though it can be only used in specific problems, it makes multiplication with larger arrays of 9 a breeze. This is illustrated with an example below. Assume you want to multiply 25 with 99.

Step 1: Subtract 1 from the dividend. 25 - 1 = 24. This is the left side of your answer.

Step 2: Subtract the result of this with the array of 9. 99 – 24 = 75. This is the right side of your answer, making it 2475.

Any similar multiplication can thus be reduced to just two steps, both of which merely involve simple subtraction.

Sutra 15: Gunitasamuchyah (The product of the sum is equal to the sum of the product)

Like the earlier sutras, this one is also used for problems relating to simultaneous equations. However, instead of solving them, it verifies whether the left and right-hand sides of the equation are indeed equal. For example, let's say you want to verify $(x + 3)(x + 2) = x^2 + 5x + 6$. The procedure for doing so is this.

Step 1: Make a note of all the coefficients of x on both sides of the equation. In this example, these are 1, 1, 1, and 5.

Step 2: In accordance with the translation of the sutra, the product of these coefficients must equal their sum. Replace the x's in the given equation, and replace it with the coefficient if it doesn't already have one. This converts the equation to $(1 + 3)(1 + 2) = 1 + 5 + 6$. Further distilled, this yields $12 = 12$. Since both sides are equal, the original equation was correct.

Sutra 16: Gunakasamuchyah (The factors of the sum are equal to the sum of the factors)

This last sutra is also meant to solve simultaneous equations. Given an equation of the form $ax^2 + bx + c = (x + d)(x + e)$, the sutra says that d and e (to avoid confusion, keep in mind that *c*, *d* and *e* are simply stand-ins for constant values; they are NOT variables like *x*—the example below will clarify this) are factors of c, and the value of d and e combined is equal to c. For example, consider the equation $x^2 + 5x + 4 = (x + 4)(x + 1)$. 4 and 1 are factors of c on the left-hand side (4), and 4 + 1 = 5, which is the coefficient of x on the left side. This shows that the equation is correct.

Takeaways

Vedic math is a system of arithmetic that is radically different from the one we have grown up learning. Despite being derived from religious scriptures that are among the oldest known to man, these rules of math remain relevant in our modern application of the discipline in several different ways. Vedic math resolves many of the commonly known gripes with the subject as we study it today.

Modern math is often perceived to be a bloated mass of different concepts glued together, with tedious processes that aren't intuitive enough to come naturally to us. In contrast, the Vedic math system was developed to be an extraordinary unity comprising only sixteen simple sutras that exhaust the breadth of mathematical problems known to us. While devoid of geometry, it covers arithmetic, algebra, statistics, and many other sub-fields of math.

Familiarizing yourself with the Vedic architecture of arithmetic inevitably involves learning and memorizing its sixteen sutras. Though these may seem convoluted at first, their application is simple and intuitive in a way that is unknown in modern math. Once you've done this, the next step is simply to learn how to apply which sutra for which problem.

You can even combine different sutras for the same problem, but each individual sutra has fairly specific applications that need to be adhered to. After you've learned how to identify particular types of problems with the corresponding sutra that can be used to simplify them, math will become infinitely easier and efficient for even those who are most unfamiliar with the subject.

Vedic math will significantly reduce the time you take to solve individual problems, which is especially beneficial in competitive examinations where time is often a luxury. Lastly, the Vedic system also acts as a powerful force for renewing interest in a discipline that has been so vilified in our society. If you find yourself struggling with the way modern math operates, Vedic math might just be the answer to your problems.

Chapter 5. The Trachtenberg System

The Trachtenberg system was developed by a man named Jakow Trachtenberg, founder of the Mathematical Institute in Zurich, Switzerland. This system relies on operations and methods that radically diverge from the ones we are accustomed to through conventional mathematics, especially since it dispenses with long and tedious multiplication tables and division. The only requirements of learning this system are knowing how to count, and memorizing certain keys that will enable you to read numbers in a way similar to letters, thereby simplifying mathematics tremendously.

Professor Trachtenberg was convinced that the reason so many of us struggle at math is not because numbers are inherently more difficult to comprehend than words, but due to the outdated and inefficient learning techniques used to teach this discipline.

The Educational Testing Service of Princeton University conducted a study over a year which revealed that not only is math the most poorly taught subject across schools in the country, but there has been no positive progress in developing better teaching methods in the past century.

The study further claimed that important discoveries made in the field since the seventeenth century have not been utilized to enhance teaching methods throughout our high schools. The result of this laggard progress has been devastating for many students.

To illustrate the depth of this quandary, one engineering school found that 72% of its students were so incompetent in math that they were forced to take refresher courses in high school math before proceeding to the regular freshman course offered by the school. Given the increasing need for trained scientists with an intuitive grasp of mathematics, these developments are particularly unfortunate. Part of the reason behind this incompetence in mathematics is the revulsion many students feel for the discipline, an attitude that has been ingrained into them since elementary and secondary school. These students generally avoid math as far as possible, eliminating the chance of them transforming into budding engineers or scientists.

The Trachtenberg system aims to reverse these ingrained attitudes by starting at the most basic arithmetic, where students first begin to feel abhorrence toward the subject. As students find themselves steadily progressing to not only perform basic calculations, but also more complex ones, they find their fear of math receding too. This system destroys the emotional roadblocks that are crucial in preventing holistic mathematical learning that improves skills and teaches students to enjoy the subject.

The use of shortcuts greatly improves students' cognitive capacity when it comes to math; this was proved in an experiment involving the armed forces during the most recent war. Bombardiers and navigators successfully learned several years' worth of mathematics in just a few months when conventional arithmetic was simplified for them through the Trachtenberg system, indicating that it really does enhance learning.

In yet another impressive testament to the benefits of learning the Trachtenberg system, students in Zurich familiar with the system competed against machines to establish which group was more proficient in math. Over an hour, the examiner narrated complicated problems involving various mathematical subtopics such as division, massive additions, complex squaring and root sums, and colossal multiplication problems.

Not only did the students complete their set of problems quicker, they were more accurate than the machines. The students chosen to participate in this test weren't geniuses either. It was the Trachtenberg system that most definitively influenced their victory over the machines.

So we now know that the Trachtenberg system simplifies math and makes it more efficient. But so does the Vedic math system. The question then is: why should one bother to learn both Vedic math, and the Trachtenberg system?

There are many benefits to both, and the choice may really boil down to personal preference. Nonetheless, we will lay down the key features of both these systems so you'll have more basis in choosing the best method to suit you.

Some of the most important benefits of the Trachtenberg system, like Vedic math, are its role in improving calculation speeds, accuracy of results, and the ease with which students perform these calculations. These are factors that characterize the method's practicality in terms of everyday use.

However, the degree of improvement in terms of re-learning and improving on your math skills is crucial for the sake of this book's mission—this is what we should be looking for first and foremost. So in terms of improved performance, educators have discovered that this system shortens time spans for computations by as much as 20%. Not only does it improve speeds by up to a fifth compared to conventional math, it assures a staggering 99% accuracy if followed correctly.

So why should we opt to learn and eventually employ the Trachtenberg system?

For one thing, given that the Trachtenberg system is known as the "shorthand of mathematics," following its procedures to the T is easier than most others like it. Similar to Vedic math, the system proposed by Trachtenberg is structured in a way that feels whole and interconnected, as opposed to the disorganized mass of normal arithmetic. It enables students completely lacking in mathematical aptitude to have the confidence and the actual capacity to be as adept at the subject as geniuses with natural technical abilities.

This system has been so effective in improving the performance of students that eventually its benefits were appreciated beyond the four walls of the academe. Owing mainly to how intuitive the system is, the Swiss have started to utilize it in all of their banks and in a majority of large businesses, as well as in their tax departments.

The revolutionary influence of this system for education and the sciences is believed by many educators to parallel the potential that shorthand possessed for business. Given the very positive reception of the public backed by substantial results; it's worth our time to check this method out and see where our quest for better mathematical performance will take us.

Lastly, the simplicity of the Trachtenberg system encourages the use of mathematics not just to solve complex equations in the classroom, but in the activities and routines that make up our everyday lives as a whole. Be it stock market quotations, monthly bills, bank statements, lotteries, calorie counting, income tax, or any other operation involving numbers, math is a part of existence as we know it, and this system can help you with any math problem you'll encounter.

The Trachtenberg system helps one simplify all the various types of numbers and computations we are confronted with on a daily basis and reduce any inconvenience they might cause us. As such, while learning the intricacies of this system will doubtless help you complete your examinations faster and more accurately, it also makes life in general much simpler than we're used to.

So without further ado, we should go ahead with learning the nitty-gritty of the Trachtenberg system.

Multiplication using the Trachtenberg System

Multiplying two digits with two digits

To provide an approachable introduction into the world of Trachtenberg's system, we will first venture out with a simple multiplication involving two-digit numbers. Write the two numbers you want to multiply in the following format:

0023 x 14

When multiplying any number with a two-digit number, always insert two zeros in the manner illustrated above. As a general rule, add as many zeros as there are digits in the multiplier. The answer to this question will be noted in the space below the first number, and the purpose of these zeroes will become clearer as we proceed. To solve this equation, utilize the steps described below:

Step 1: Multiply the two digits at the extreme right of the two respective numbers. In this case, these are 3 and 4. 3 x 4 = 12. Note the 2 from the product 12 below the digit 3, and mark it with an asterisk (*) as illustrated here:

0023 x 14

   *2

Step 2: This step requires you to perform two minor calculations. First, multiply the digit to the left of the one on the extreme right with the outermost digit of your multiplier. Here, these are 2 and 4 respectively. 2 x 4 = 8. Second, multiply the remaining two numbers, 3 and 1, to obtain 3. Add the two numbers thus derived. 8 + 3 = 11. Add the one you carried over from before to make 11 + 1 = 12. This will be denoted exactly as we did in step 1.

0023 x 14

*2 *2

Step 3: Now multiply the leftmost figures (not counting the zeros) of the two numbers, here 2 and 1. 2 x 1 = 2, and add the 1 carried over from before to make it 3.

0023 x 14

3*2*2

322 is the correct answer. To recap the whole process, we first multiplied the rightmost digits of the two numbers together (that is 3 and 4). Then, to find the extreme left digit of the answer, we multiplied the leftmost digits (2 and 1) and accounted for any number that was carried over. Lastly, to find the middle digit, we noted two pairs, one of the outermost numbers (2 and 4) and the other comprising the innermost ones (3 and 1). We then added the result of the two multiplications.

Multiplying any number with a two-digit number

We will now use the same process described earlier to multiply a number of any length with a two-digit number. Assume you want to multiply 312 by 14.

00312 x 14

Step 1: Multiply the rightmost digits of the two numbers, here 2 and 4. 2 x 4 = 8.

00312 x 14
    8

Step 2: Now denote the outermost and innermost pairs. Since the next digit of the answer is supposed to be noted below the 1 in 00312, it is part of the outermost pair in this equation. Two pairs are thus 4 and 1, along with 2 and 1. Multiply the two pairs together. 4 x 1 = 4 and 2 x 1 = 2. Add the two together to obtain 6 (4 + 2).

00312 x 14
    68

Step 3: This step is a repetition of the previous one, albeit with different pairs. Since the next digit of the answer is to be noted below 3 in 00312, 3 is part of the outermost pair in this step. Thus, the two pairs here are 3 and 4, along with 1 and 1. Multiply the two pairs together. 3 x 4 = 12 and 1 x 1 = 1. Add the two together to obtain 13 (12 + 1). Note the 3 of 13 below the 3 in 00312 with an asterisk to symbolize the 1 that needs to be carried over.

00312 x 14
  *368 x 14

Step 4: Now simply multiply the leftmost digits in the two numbers to obtain the last digit of the answer. 3 x 1 = 3, and add the 1 carried over from before to obtain 4. 4368 is the correct answer.

Multiplying a number with a 3-digit number

Let's assume you want to multiply 213 and 121. Since the multiplier (121) has three digits, add three zeros in your denotation:

000213 x 121.

Step 1: Multiply the rightmost digits of the two numbers, here 3 and 1. 3 x 1 = 3.

000213 x 121

    3

Step 2: Multiply the innermost and outermost pairs as we did in the previous example. To recount, since the next digit of the answer must be noted below the 1 in 000213, 1 is part of the outermost pair. Thus, the pairs are 1 and 1, along with 3 and 2. Multiply the two together and add the results. 1 x 1 = 1 and 3 x 2 = 6. 6 + 1 = 7. 7 is the next digit of your answer.

000213 x 121

73

Step 3: Diverging from the procedure followed before, we now need to form three pairs of numbers. However, the process of determining them is the same. The outermost numbers are now 2 and 1, which forms the first pair. The other two pairs are 1 and 2, along with 3 and 1. Multiply all three pairs together and add the results. 2 x 1 = 2, 1 x 2 = 2, and 3 x 1 = 3. 2 + 2 + 3 = 7. 7 is the third digit of your answer.

000213 x 121

773

Step 4: This step again requires us to form three pairs, but starting one place to the left of our previous position. Thus, the outermost pair now consists of 0 and 1, while the two other pairs are 2 and 2, and 1 with 1. 0 x 1 = 0, 2 x 2 = 4, and 1 x 1 = 1. Add the three numbers together to obtain 5.

000213 x 121

5773

Step 5: This is the last step of the example since the answer to the next one, if we follow the procedure of earlier steps, will inevitably be 0. Follow the same process as earlier by forming three more pairs, moving one place to the left. The three pairs are 0 and 1, 0 and 2, along with 2 and 1. Any number multiplied by zero is 0, so we only need to perform the last multiplication. 2 x 1 = 2. This is the last digit of your answer, which is 25773.

Using Multipliers of Any Length

We have progressed from an increasing numbers of multipliers and, as such, we learned how multiplication through the system works conceptually. Through that, we can now multiply two numbers of any length together following the procedures outlined above. To demonstrate, let's assume you want to multiply 2103 with 3214.

Step 1: Multiply the rightmost digits of the two numbers, 3 and 4. 3 x 4 = 12. Note the 2 and mark the 1 to be carried over with an asterisk.

00002103 x 3214

*2

Step 2: Form innermost and outermost pairs as before. 0 must be paired with 4, and 3 with 1. 3 x 1 = 3. Add the 1 carried over from before to obtain 4.

00002103 x 3214

4*2

Step 3: Keep forming pairs while moving leftward. The outermost pair now comprises 1 and 4. The other two pairs are 0 and 1, along with 3 and 2. Multiply them together. 4 x 1 = 4, 0 x 1 = 0, and 3 x 2 = 6. Add the results together to obtain 10 (6 + 4). Note the zero and carry one over for the next step.

00002103 x 3214

*04*2

Step 4: We now form four pairs, one each for every digit in the multiplier. These are 2 and 4, 1 and 1, 0 and 2, 3 and 3. Multiply them together. 2 x 4 = 8, 1 x 1 = 1, 0 x 2 = 0, 3 x 3 = 9. Add these together to obtain 18. Add the 1 to be carried over to obtain 19. Note the 9 and mark the 1 that carries on further.

00002103 x 3214

*9*04*2

Step 5: Move leftward and form four new pairs. These are 0 and 4, 2 and 1, 1 and 2, 0 and 3. Multiply them together. 0 x 4 = 0, 2 x 1 = 2, 1 x 2 = 2, and 0 x 3 = 0. Add them together to obtain 4, and add the 1 carried over from before. This yields 5.

00002103 x 3214

5*9*04*2

Step 6: The new pairs are now 0 and 4, 0 and 1, 2 and 2, 1 and 3. Multiply the last two pairs. 2 x 2 = 4 and 1 x 3 = 3. 4 + 3 = 7.

00002103 x 3214

75*9*04*2

Step 7: This is the final step since the answer to the next set of pairs will inevitably be 0. The pairs here are 0 and 4, 0 and 1, 0 and 2, and 2 with 3. Multiply the last pair to obtain 6, which is the last digit of the answer. 6759042 is the correct answer.

Addition in Trachtenberg's System

There are two notable differences in addition as performed in the Trachtenberg system and the procedure followed in conventional mathematics that we need to keep in mind. First, while the latter involves noting the problem in a way that stacks all the numbers one below the other and adding columns from right to left, the Trachtenberg system proceeds from left to right—a horizontal flow of calculation. Secondly, while the addition of individual columns can produce any number, in the system we never count higher than 11 until the very last step. What this second part says is quite obscure without the use of good examples. The meaning will become clearer as we proceed.

To take an example, let's say you want to add this series of numbers:

3689 + 758 + 9667 + 1064 + 6498 + 756 + 9968 + 5887 + 9988 + 7615 + 8749

If you were to stack these numbers together and proceed individually by column, as we would in our conventional method, it would definitely take you far too long to finish adding them up. However, this process is infinitely simplified by following the process outlined by the Trachtenberg system. As mentioned before, in this system we start from right to left, and never count higher than 11.

Step 1: Stack the numbers as you normally would in the following manner:

3689
 758
9667
1064
6498
 745
9968
5887
9988
7615
8749

Step 2: Continue adding the leftmost column from top to bottom. However, if a step increases the running total beyond 11, mark a tick at that step and subtract the result of that step by 11. For example, 3 + 9 = 12, which is more than 11. Mark a tick near 9 and subtract 11 from 12 from before proceeding to continue adding. 1 + 1 = 2, 2 + 6 = 8, and 8 + 9 = 17, which is again higher than 11. Mark a tick near 9 and subtract 11 from 17 to obtain 6 before moving on. Continue this until the column has been exhausted. The running total will finally amount to 2. Make a note of the number of ticks aggregated for each column and note them below the running total as described below:

3689
 758
9667
1064
6498
 745
9968

5887
9988
7615
8749
———
2

5

Step 3: Repeat step 2 for every column. Your final tally should be as follows:

 758
9667
1064
6498
 745
9968
5887
9988

7615

8749

———

23 10 1

56 5 7

Step 4: Now, we can deduce the final answer by adding the running totals and ticks in this way. Add every running total with the number of ticks directly below it, and the number of ticks to the right. For example, in the leftmost column, simply add 1 and 7 to yield 8. Then, moving leftward, first add 10 with 5 to obtain 15, and then add the number of ticks to the right of 5 (7). 15 + 7 = 22. Note the 2 and mark two asterisks to denote the number that needs to be carried over. In the next column, add 3 and 6 to yield 9, followed by adding 5 to 9 to yield 14. Add the two from the previous step to obtain 16. Note the 6 and mark one asterisk that needs to be carried over. Follow this until you've exhausted all columns. Add 2, 5, and 6 to obtain 13, and include the 1 carried over from the previous column to yield 14. Note the 1 that needs to be carried over.

Step 5: Since we've run out of numbers, but have a 1 that needs be carried forward, we'll include a zero in front of the rows of running totals and ticks in the following manner:

0 2 3 1 0 1 (Running totals)
0 5 6   5 7 (Ticks)

This arrangement of running totals and ticks is called the working table. Add the two zeroes with 5, and use the one carried over from before to yield 6.

Step 6: Account for all the numbers derived so far to obtain the correct answer, which is 64628.

Verifying your answer

Given the many minor steps of addition involved, even one mistake will yield you the wrong answer and leave you scrambling to find the step where you committed the error. Just imagine this happening in a situation such as an exam with a time constraint. As such, it is imperative that one be able to verify their answer without having to perform the entire set of additions all over again, and this section provides you with a method to do that.

Step 1: Find the digit sums of the two numbers. Remember, nines don't count and must be treated as a zero. For the numbers we chose in the example above, the digit sums are 8, 2 (758 = 7 + 5 + 8, which obtains 20. Add the digits of 20 to yield 2), 1, 2, 0, 7, 5, 1, 7, 1, and 1.

Step 2: Add these numbers together to obtain 35. The sum of digits in 35 yields 8. The sum of the digits in the answer, 64628, also yields 8. This proves that our answer was correct.

To summarize, the digit sums of every number you need to add, if then added together, should give you the same number as the digit sum of the answer you derived. If it doesn't, your answer is likely incorrect.

Division in the Trachtenberg System

The method of division used here, known as the *simple method*, requires no prior knowledge of mathematics besides simple addition and subtraction. To demonstrate this method with an example, let's assume you want to divide 27,483,624 by 62. Instead of following the tediously slow long division method, consider the steps described below:

Step 1: Make two columns, one named the "*Check column*" and the other the "*Divisor column*." The dividend is the larger number in a problem involving division, while the divisor is the number it needs to be divided by. The divisor column consists of the divisor, 62 in this case, being added 10 times with itself, while the check column starts with the sum of the digits in a divisor being added up. They initially look as described below:

Check Column   Divisor Column

 8   62
+8   +62

Step 2: In the divisor column, keep adding 62 ten times just as you would perform simple addition in conventional math. In the check column, add the number derived from adding the digits of the divisor with itself right beside the divisor column. Performing the first addition should yield the following result:

Check Column   Divisor Column

```
   8              62
  +8             +62
  ——             ——-
  16             124
```

Every time you obtain a number in the check column that is 10 or more, convert it into single digits by adding up the digits comprising the number. If you encounter a 9, convert it into a 0. In this case, since 16 is more than 9, add 1 and 6 to yield 7 and note it as described:

Check Column   Divisor Column

```
   8              62
  +8             +62
  ——             ——-
 (16)—>7         124
```

Step 3: Continue adding the sum of the divisor's digits in the check column and reduce every two-digit occurrence to a single digit one. Similarly, continue adding the divisor column with 62 after every addition in the divisor column. Label every second step as shown below:

Divisor Column

62 (1)

+62

——-

124 (2)

+62

——-

186 (3)

+62

——-

248 (4)

Repeat the iterative steps of addition in both columns until you have performed ten sets of addition each. The result of these additions is given below:

Check Column Dividend	Divisor Column Answer
8	62
27483624	
+8	+62
——	——-
16=7	124 (2)
+8	+62
——	——-
15=6	186 (3)
+8	+62
——-	——-

14=5 +8 ——— 	248 (4) +62 ———
13=4 +8 ———	310 (5) +62 ———
12=3 +8 ———	372 (6) +62 ———
11=2 +8 ———	434 (7) +62 ———
10=1 +8 ———	496 (8) +62 ———
9=0 +8 ——— 8	558 (9) +62 ——— 620

To double-check your additions in the divisor column, notice how the digits of every labeled step in the column correspond to the value derived on the left in the check column. For example, in (2), the digits of 124 add up to 7, which is the sum of the digits in 16 that was deduced in the column on the left.

Step 4: Now start considering the digits in the dividend starting from the extreme left. We need to find numbers in the divisor column that we can subtract from the digits of the dividend. Since the divisor is a two-digit number, we'll consider the first two digits of the dividend, 27. However, there is no number lower than 27 in the entire divisor column, so we'll bring in an additional digit from the dividend, making the number 274. Which number in the divisor column is closest and lower than 274? It's 248 in (4). Note 248 below the digits 274 in the dividend column drawn above and perform a simple subtraction. Next, write 4 from the label (4) in the answer column. This is the first digit of your final answer.

Step 5: Once you've performed the first subtraction, bring the next digit from the dividend down and search for the next closest and lower number. 274 – 248 = 26, and the next digit is 8, making the number 268. The closest number is again 248, so we repeat the subtraction as before and add another 4 in the answer column. Repeat this step until all the digits in the dividend have been exhausted. The answer should look as follows:

27483624   Answer: 443284
248 (4)
———
  268
  248 (4)
————
   203
   186 (3)

─ ─ ─ ─

   176

   124 (2)

─ ─ ─ ─

   522

   496 (8)

─ ─ ─ ─

   264

   248 (4)

─ ─ ─ ─

   16

16 is the remainder in this case, while 443284 is the quotient.

Takeaways

Like Vedic math, the Trachtenberg system is yet another unique set of procedures for performing complex calculations in a way that is far more intuitive and simple than conventional arithmetic. Developed by

Jakow Trachtenberg in Zurich, it was specifically designed to revolutionize the way we learn and comprehend numbers along with their accompanying operational signs.

However, sadly enough, math as a discipline has remained stagnant for centuries now as new developments in the field routinely fail to percolate down to our classrooms. As such, the way we are taught math often uses procedures from the 17th century or earlier, with knowledge of more recent techniques confined to the academic community of mathematicians—or perhaps a tutorial company promoting yet another fad in teaching. However, the Trachtenberg system changes that by offering an altogether new way of doing math that will appeal to many who have traditionally struggled with the subject.

Though this system offers many of the same benefits as Vedic math, it has one crucial advantage over the latter. Instead of having to learn sutras in Sanskrit and scrambling to identify which sutra is applicable for which problem, the Trachtenberg system offers a different solution. Its methods are uniform in that its procedure for multiplication or division can be used for any problem which involves these operations.

Though it demands that you re-learn everything about math as you know it, this system also promises many benefits in return. Among these are an uncomplicated and clean process for solving problems that manages to save significant amounts of time for the individual using it. Studies have found that those using the Trachtenberg system can perform calculations quicker than machines, and increase their calculation speeds by up to a fifth compared to conventional math. Furthermore, this system makes for an alternative way of doing arithmetic that is much more suitable for those who generally struggle with the subject.

Summary Guide

Chapter 1. "I *hate* math!"
It is no secret that math is among the most reviled subjects taught to us in school. There are many reasons for this, from poor teaching methods, to the impression that the subject lacks practical applicability, and the ever-present choice of simply using a calculator instead. The extent of our hatred for math has reached such heights that math anxiety is now a commonly recognized phenomenon wherein just the prospect of having to do math causes adverse mental and physiological symptoms.

All of these factors have combined to make math skills a reason to be socially ostracized. Math is perceived to be a subject only fit for the nerdiest of nerds. It just isn't cool, and if one is good at it, their analytical acumen is thought to be a sign of abnormality. The result of such attitudes is that mathematical ability is perceived to be a purely natural skill that one is either born with in spades, or has been robbed of due to the vagaries of cosmic justice. Students who struggle with math are stuck believing they are doomed to be unsuccessful at the subject no matter how much effort they put into improving their skills.

Teachers are thus tasked with reversing the trend and inculcating a growth mindset in their students by normalizing failure and providing ample encouragement instead of derision. When children are placed in supportive teaching environments that don't punish them for an inability to solve every problem, while also providing them with innovative and interesting ways to learn, their attitudes toward math change. Their improvements reinforce the belief that math is something anybody can excel at when provided with the necessary resources.

Chapter 2. Mental Math in Daily Life

The lack of obvious practical applications is at the heart of disinterest in studying and excelling at math for many who are struggling at the subject. Due to the way we are taught the subject in school, most of us fail to see how we can find x outside the problems listed in our textbooks. Yet math pervades almost every sphere of our practical life in unique and wondrous ways. If we want to cook something, we need math to measure and use the right amount of ingredients.

If we wish to manage our finances efficiently, especially when it involves accounting for the value of fluctuating stocks and the income lost to taxes, we need several different mathematical operations to do so. Even if we just want to decide how much to tip the waiter at a restaurant we visit, we need to be familiar with concepts like percentages. As such, math is practically unavoidable in our daily lives, so it pays to be familiar with at least its most basic concepts.

It is true that we always have the option of relying on the internet or calculators to do our math for us, but no tool can help us if we don't know the procedure for calculating whatever it is we need to find out. Calculators don't input the numbers and operations by themselves; it is we who need to provide them with that data. Yet once we discover how simple it is to perform most of the operations we need in our daily lives, the need for calculators disappears altogether.

There are several mental math tricks which can help you deduce answers in a matter of seconds for a wide variety of applications. Not only will these tricks make you appear intelligent in the company of your peers, being able to do them fills you with a sense of achievement unlike anything else.

Chapter 3. Calculations

The overwhelming majority of the arithmetic we need to learn for routine tasks such as cooking, tipping, calculating our grades, and managing finances all boils down to becoming competently efficient at the five key operations. These are addition, subtraction, multiplication, division, and percentages.

Expressing numbers in different forms, such as fractions and decimals, also figures into this discussion because, essentially, these are but other ways that we can express percentages.

As we've gotten to know the behavior of the numerical forms through their interaction with these arithmetic operations, it is tempting to assume they are simple enough that there's no need for more extensive study. It might seem like all we need is a little brushing up on the basics, along with some paper or perhaps a calculator. Paradoxically enough, this kind of mindset could coexist with the math aversion mindset mentioned early on.

Nonetheless, as the saying goes, there is more than one way to skin a cat. There are many different ways we can use the five aforementioned concepts to our advantage. Depending on one's preferences and the techniques that come naturally to them, we can choose from several equally valid procedures to solve a problem. In line with this book's goal, we want to become confident enough to do the math necessary for our everyday affairs. But beyond that, we are also aspiring to a level of improvement that will further develop our cognitive capacities. Hence, the approach that fortifies our mental math abilities.

The beauty of mental math is that we can perform every single one of these procedures using our mind alone, without needing pens, papers, or calculators. In many instances, we don't require answers that are accurate to the last decimal digit.

Approximations suffice, and serve our purposes adequately. Regardless of which method you choose to pursue, the secret to achieving the right answer, whether precise or approximate, is in the ability to convert complex calculations into ones that are more easily comprehensible. In other words, we address these problems by breaking them down to manageable portions.

For example, if you need to multiply something by 11, multiply the number by

10 instead and simply add the number to your product. This is but one of the many ways to reduce problems that seem too complicated to solve in our minds into ones that can be simplified in seconds. Having said that, most of the calculations we are confronted with in our daily lives are fairly simple, and can easily be tackled with just five concepts from the world of math.

Chapter 4. Vedic Math

Vedic math is a system of arithmetic that is radically different from the one we have grown up learning. Despite being derived from religious scriptures that are among the oldest known to man, these rules of math remain relevant in our modern application of the discipline in several different ways. Vedic math resolves many of the commonly known gripes with the subject as we study it today.

Modern math is often perceived to be a bloated mass of different concepts glued together, with tedious processes that aren't intuitive enough to come naturally to us. In contrast, the Vedic math system was developed to be an extraordinary unity comprising only sixteen simple sutras that exhaust the breadth of mathematical problems known to us. While devoid of geometry, it covers arithmetic, algebra, statistics, and many other sub-fields of math.

Familiarizing yourself with the Vedic architecture of arithmetic inevitably involves learning and memorizing its sixteen sutras. Though these may seem convoluted at first, their application is simple and intuitive in a way that is unknown in modern math. Once you've done this, the next step is simply to learn how to apply which sutra for which problem.

You can even combine different sutras for the same problem, but each individual sutra has fairly specific applications that need to be adhered to. After you've learned how to identify particular types of problems with the corresponding sutra that can be used to simplify them, math will become infinitely easier and efficient for even those who are most unfamiliar with the subject.

Vedic math will significantly reduce the time you take to solve individual problems, which is especially beneficial in competitive examinations where time is often a luxury. Lastly, the Vedic system also acts as a powerful force for renewing interest in a discipline that has been so vilified in our society. If you find yourself struggling with the way modern math operates, Vedic math might just be the answer to your problems.

Chapter 5. The Trachtenberg System

Like Vedic math, the Trachtenberg system is yet another unique set of procedures for performing complex calculations in a way that is far more intuitive and simple than conventional arithmetic. Developed by Jakow Trachtenberg in Zurich, it was specifically designed to revolutionize the way we learn and comprehend numbers along with their accompanying operational signs.

However, sadly enough, math as a discipline has remained stagnant for centuries now as new developments in the field routinely fail to percolate down to our classrooms. As such, the way we are taught math often uses procedures from the 17th century or earlier, with knowledge of more recent techniques confined to the academic community of mathematicians—or perhaps a tutorial company promoting yet another fad in teaching. However, the Trachtenberg system changes that by offering an altogether new way of doing math that will appeal to many who have traditionally struggled with the subject.

Though this system offers many of the same benefits as Vedic math, it has one crucial advantage over the latter. Instead of having to learn sutras in Sanskrit and scrambling to identify which sutra is applicable for which problem, the Trachtenberg system offers a different solution. Its methods are uniform in that its procedure for multiplication or division can be used for any problem which involves these operations.

Though it demands that you re-learn everything about math as you know it, this system also promises many benefits in return. Among these are an uncomplicated and clean process for solving problems that manages to save significant amounts of time for the individual using it. Studies have found that those using the Trachtenberg system can perform calculations quicker than machines, and increase their calculation speeds by up to a fifth compared to conventional math. Furthermore, this system makes for an alternative way of doing arithmetic that is much more suitable for those who generally struggle with the subject.

www.ingramcontent.com/pod-product-compliance
Lightning Source LLC
Chambersburg PA
CBHW071344080526
44587CB00017B/2959